the
diversity
gap

the diversity gap

Where Good Intentions Meet True Cultural Change

Bethaney Wilkinson

HarperCollins
Leadership

AN IMPRINT OF HARPERCOLLINS

Published by HarperCollins Leadership, an imprint of HarperCollins Focus LLC.

Book design by Maria Fernandez for Neuwirth & Associates.

Any internet addresses, phone numbers, or company or product information printed in this book are offered as a resource and are not intended in any way to be or to imply an endorsement by HarperCollins Leadership, nor does HarperCollins Leadership vouch for the existence, content, or services of these sites, phone numbers, companies, or products beyond the life of this book.

ISBN 978-1-4002-2629-0 (eBook)
ISBN 978-1-4002-2623-8 (HC)

Library of Congress Control Number: 2021942458

Printed in the United States of America
21 22 23 24 25 LSC 10 9 8 7 6 5 4 3 2 1

To Bishop and Janet,

whose faithful legacy of impact and love will carry on for generations

CONTENTS

When a flower doesn't bloom, you fix the environment in which it grows, not the flower.

—Alexander Den Heijer

WORDS YOU
NEED TO KNOW

DIVERSITY

The state of having multiple races, ethnicities, nationalities, and cultural perspectives on your team.

INCLUSION

The experience of being welcomed and of authentic belonging.

RECONCILIATION

The ongoing process of restoring authentic and mutually dignifying relationships among people from different racial, ethnic, and cultural perspectives.

LIBERATION

Freedom from oppressive systems, stories, habits, policies, and practices.

CULTURE OF THE FUTURE

An organizational environment in which people from racially, ethnically, and culturally diverse backgrounds are heard, seen, uplifted, and supported at work.

An organizational culture in which leaders consistently and authentically disrupt systems of oppression.

THE DIVERSITY GAP

The distance between our good intentions for creating diverse organizations and the impact of those intentions.

AUTHOR'S NOTE

One of the most significant decisions I had to make in writing this book was choosing how to identify and label various racial groups. This topic is widely debated. Here is where I've landed for now:

I've chosen to capitalize the names of specific racial groups when referring to the people they identify and represent—for example, Asian, Black, White, Indigenous, and so on.

I've chosen not to capitalize "white" and "black" when referring to institutions, systemic realities (e.g., white supremacy, white privilege, antiblack racism), and oppressive social groups (e.g., white nationalists).

I've also chosen not to capitalize broad racial groups inclusive of varied and diverse peoples, perspectives, and experiences (e.g., multiracial, biracial, people of color).

When quoting or referring to specific individuals and their ideas, I identify them however they label or identify themselves. I capitalize or do not capitalize these identifiers according to their preference.

Each of these choices reflects a degree of generalization. As a rule, I value specificity, but generalizations make this conversation more accessible in the format of a book. Maybe one day, we can sit across from one another and hold a specific conversation. Until then, I hope these categories and stylistic decisions will do.

Introduction

YOU ARE CREATING THE FUTURE

I'm writing this book because, in my eight short years of working in majority white, values-driven institutions, I've experienced a level of organizational heartache I didn't know was possible. This heartache brought with it all the fixtures of a romantic breakup: countless tears, sleepless nights, confusion from unmet expectations, and, of course, a broken heart. I entered the workforce at age twenty-two with wide-open eyes and hopeful visions to change the world. I prioritized working in values-driven, charitable institutions. I believed in the value of service and in our social responsibility to care for those on the margins. I wanted to be part of something bigger than myself, so I aligned my efforts with nonprofits, churches, and social enterprises.

Over time, despite my optimism, I found myself lonely, anxious, and depressed as I navigated the organizational cultures of "do-good" institutions clearly not designed with me—a young Black woman—in mind.

I experienced microaggressions on a regular basis. I was overlooked for promotions, because I wasn't perceived to be enough of a "go-getter," despite my loyalty and hard work. When race-related issues *did* emerge in our work context, I became responsible for educating everyone, while also tending to my own race-related trauma. When I made suggestions for how we could be more inclusive of different racial perspectives, I was either argued with or my recommendations were ignored. In the heat of a racial crisis, I would be asked to weigh in on communications decisions to make sure our messaging was "woke" enough, but when I advocated for comprehensive racial justice programming, it either "wasn't in the budget," "wasn't a priority," or "the calendar was too full."

These experiences were pervasive. They did not unfold in one work setting or in one organization—this was my experience in multiple workplaces and on multiple teams. Ironically, I consistently found myself in rooms with leaders who would affirm their desire to have a more diverse organization, yet, as the only Black person on the team, I regularly felt disempowered and disrespected in these environments.

I started to wonder, *Am I losing my mind? Is it me? Am I alone in this?*

With these deeply personal questions and organizational frustrations in mind, I set out to explore this gap between people's good intentions for diversity and the impact of those intentions. Leaders with good intentions were a dime a dozen; leaders with good impact, especially good impact on underrepresented racial minorities, were few and far between. I wanted to know why.

Over the past two years, I've interviewed more than a hundred thought leaders, diversity and inclusion experts, creatives, authors, and entrepreneurs about organizational culture and diversity. I've talked to people from a wide variety of racial backgrounds. I've learned from people at different levels of organizational leadership. I've attended events, hosted conversations, created a podcast, and more. I've wrapped my life around questions of organizational culture and diversity.

While I've been exposed to many perspectives on this topic, I've come to realize that the most significant perspective I have to offer you is my own observations and stories based on thirty years of lived experience as a Black person navigating life in the United States. When your story is filled with moments as "the first," "the only," and "the different," you quickly learn what exclusion feels like. However, you also acquire a strong sense of knowing what makes true inclusion possible.

When I was twenty-three years old and leaving my first job at an all-white organization, I gave them in parting a list of areas they would need to shift if they aspired to create a racially diverse organization. I poured my heart and soul into that list for two reasons. The first reason was because I felt responsible for telling the truth about what needed to change in order to create an environment where someone like me (a Black person) would want to be. The second reason I wrote the list was because I believed in those leaders; I trusted them. I hoped if I shared a perspective they didn't have, but desperately needed, they would make changes so people of color would have better workplace experiences in the future.

I wrote this book for those same reasons.

1. I feel a responsibility to tell the truth about what needs to change in majority white organizations aspiring to be more racially and ethnically diverse.
2. I believe the leaders of today have a responsibility to make changes so future generations can experience the gifts of racial and ethnic diversity, and avoid the tears, sleepless nights, confusion, and brokenheartedness that is part and parcel to the experiences of so many of people of color in organizations today.

This book you are holding is a collection of the eight insights I wish I could have told every White boss, supervisor, and well-meaning leader before they hired me. These are the eight insights I want every leader, inclusive of all racial and ethnic identities, to have if they aspire to create a racially and ethnically diverse organization. I've curated this list because I've seen and experienced many instances where "diversity work" goes horribly wrong. I'm hopeful we can do better.

The eight insights (and accompanying chapters) are:

1. Your team's lack of "racial diversity is not the root of the problem. Racism and white supremacy are the root problems. Adjust your perspective and strategies accordingly.
2. The impact of your organizational culture on people of color is more important than your good intentions. Prioritize hearing, believing, and following people of color.

3. Your motivation for diversifying your team matters. If this is about dignifying people, keep going. If this is about appearing relevant, stop now.

4. There are many frameworks for pursuing organizational culture and diversity, and each has different objectives. Choose your framework and know why.

5. You have to adopt new, and more liberating, values and behaviors if you want diverse groups of people to flourish as they follow you. Practice liberation; embody cultural change.

6. Your ability to cultivate a diverse personal life is directly tied to your ability to lead a diverse team. Resist racism and pursue diversity in every area of your life.

7. People don't just want a job; people want to belong. Your intentionality and vulnerability set the tone for how much belonging is possible. Lead with courage.

8. No one is asking you to be perfect. We are asking you to get uncomfortable, be creative, take some risks, and show up with consistency. You have to do your work.

Our action and inaction today are creating the workplace environments of tomorrow. We are creating the cultures of the future. In my imagination, I fast-forward to the day when I have children, and they eventually set out to chase their dreams. When my kids show up to their first job, I want them to work for leaders who will amplify their voices and not diminish their light. I want the future to be a better, more inclusive, and more equitable place not only for my future family, but for all of us. As leaders, creating the cultures of the future is our responsibility. Closing diversity gaps, near and far, is our challenge and our opportunity.

In the pages to follow, I am going to unpack each of these eight insights with stories, metaphors, diagrams, opinions, and more. At the end of the book, you will find a series of group-reflection questions for each chapter, as well as exercises. The best way to work through this resource is to read it with anyone who coleads, comanages, or codirects your organization. This might be your board of directors or your executive leadership team. If you are currently leading a majority white organization, this resource is even *more* important as you determine how much you are truly willing to invest in change.

I hope you are challenged and inspired by what you find in these pages. I also hope you discover a path toward increasing racial diversity that not only works for you, but affirms the dignity of Black people, Indigenous people, multiracial people, and people of color everywhere.

Our work is cut out for us.

Let's get to it.

RACISM
IS THE PROBLEM

- *Insight:* Your team's lack of racial diversity is not the root problem. Racism and white supremacy are the root problems.

- *Action:* Take inventory of how racism and white supremacy exist within your culture. Adjust your diversity strategy to disrupt these systems.

ORIGIN STORIES

Where did you come from? Where does your story begin? What is your origin story?

Origin stories are narratives telling us who we are, where we are from, and why we exist. They also tell us who our community is, who our heroes and villains are, and what it takes to participate meaningfully in the world around us.

• • ● • • •

Racism and white supremacy are the root problems.

• • ● • • •

Our origin stories determine so many aspects of our lives and our leadership. We bring these origin stories to work, to the cultures we create, to the organizations we design, and to the teams we build.

When I think of my origin story, my heart and mind go to places I've only heard stories about. I think of my father and his grandfather hunting in southern woods when he was a boy. I think of my mother and her mother cooking and eating neck bones. Going back even further, I think of cotton fields and long days in the heat of the sun. I think of shotgun houses, gravel roads, red clay, and dusty days. I think of the peanut factory where my great-grandfather worked, and the long nights my grandmother spent cleaning hospitals to make ends meet for her family. I think of resiliency, creativity, a deeply ingrained work ethic, and a whole lot of love.

This is my origin story, the beginnings of a young Black woman born and raised in the southern United States. I've heard it said, "We speak from where our feet stand."[1] I would also say, "We *lead* from where our feet stand." From the places we were born, from the families and communities that shaped us, from the stories we were told about who we are and what life is all about, our origin stories impact everything about how we lead.

Another formative detail of my origin story has a lot to do with the terror of racism. I didn't experience chattel slavery or life during Jim Crow, but the trauma of such experiences lives in our bodies and gets passed on through generations.[2] It never goes away; it just changes form. Societally, the violence and oppression White bodies inflicted upon Black bodies morphed from chattel slavery to Jim Crow terrorism to economic exploitation and political oppression to mass incarceration and the criminalization of poverty—same violence, ever-evolving forms.

These age-old evils aren't new to readers in the twenty-first century, and the purpose of this book isn't to unpack the long-standing and historical legacy of antiblack racism in the United States. This is a book about leadership and what each of us can do to close diversity gaps and create diverse, liberating cultures for the future. After many years in racial justice education and, most recently, time spent interviewing people about the gap between good intentions for diversity and the impact of those intentions, here's what we know:

In the next few pages, I will unpack the meaning of racism and white supremacy, because they are at the root of organizational challenges to racially and ethnically diverse teams—especially if we seek to diversify with dignity. I want to ground your learning through this book in a working understanding of these definitions and realities so you can move toward imagining a new way, bridging the gap between your intentions and your impact in leadership and life.

We must begin where our feet stand by peeling back the layers of our origin stories to discover the impact of race, racism, and white supremacy on who we are, what we create, and how we lead.

A CRACK IN
THE FOUNDATION

Have you ever built a house before? Chances are, like me, your answer is no. But in recent months, I've learned a great deal about what it takes to build one. My husband and I purchased one acre of land filled with wild grasses and flowers, as well as pecan, cedar, sweet gum, and mulberry trees. It also had a house that was no longer inhabitable because it burned down earlier in the year. Our plan was to tear down the old house and build our own.

As we began learning about what it takes to build a home, we were repeatedly asked if the foundation of the old house was still intact. As new home builders, it was apparent that a good foundation was a big deal. A strong and secure foundation is where every good home begins. Any weaknesses or cracks in the foundation would compromise the structural integrity of the home.

When I step back and look at the origin stories of many companies and organizations in the United States, racism and white supremacy exist as pervasive cracks in the foundation. Like an old house, these cracks are not always visible in the beginning; we only know there is a problem over time, when the earth shifts and the storms come. In these critical moments, we can see the problem for what it is.

As you reflect on your personal or organizational origin story, are there any cracks in the foundation? These could be tiny fissures, practically unseen by the human eye, or large, obvious cracks that need immediate attention.

Here are three leadership stories to illustrate how racism and white supremacy emerge as cracks in the foundation of good intentions toward creating racially, ethnically, and culturally diverse teams.

Story #1

The theme of the conference was "uncommon fellowship." I was excited about the event for one reason: there was a stellar lineup of racial justice champions set to be on the mainstage. It was 2016 and, everywhere I looked, communities were struggling with what to do about race, racism, and the political division running rampant on social media feeds and in the daily news. This leadership conference appeared to be tackling the tension head-on.

As the event got underway, however, I was struck by how many White men took the stage. The primary voices setting the tone for the conversation were from the majority culture. Typically, Black people, Indigenous people, and people of color have a better awareness and understanding of issues related to racial unity, or the lack thereof. We have firsthand experience with the problem. And yet, I thought, *The same old voices that usually take up the most space with their presence, thoughts, and leadership were doing it all over again.*

Time progressed, and we were getting close to lunch. The moment was finally here as racial reconciliation and justice thought leaders took the stage. The first, Dr. Brenda Salter McNeil, a woman who'd dedicated more than twenty-five years to the work of racial reconciliation, was phenomenal as usual. But then, something interesting happened. Rather than the other racial justice leaders each getting the normal twenty to thirty minutes to speak, they were all folded into a panel. This was striking to me, because each of the presenters was a compelling leader and communicator in their own right. They each could have easily filled an entire talk. I was hoping to learn from all of them, so I was disappointed to find they each only had five to seven minutes to share their thoughts and opinions on this important topic.

I was so unsettled by this experience that, when I arrived home, I got online to learn more about the event planning team. Out of nearly thirty people working for this organization, only one of them was a Black person. I lived in Atlanta, Georgia, one of the most racially and ethnically diverse cities in the country. How was this planning team (nearly) all White?

Racism and white supremacy were cracks in the foundation.

Story #2

It's 2020. The United States is shaken yet again by a series of highly publicized murders of Black people in episodes of racial violence and police brutality. An uprising is underway. Businesses and organizations, large and small, are scrambling to respond. Many release statements declaring: Black Lives Matter. Many leverage their platforms to advocate for justice and change. There is a profound focus on amplifying the experiences of Black and other racially marginalized people in the world. And protests sprout up across the globe, desperately crying out for change.

I was thrilled to see so much activity and advocacy; I loved watching people from diverse backgrounds raise their voices for change. It was hopeful to hear new voices leverage their perspectives and areas of influence to make a difference. Many folks were petitioning local governments for radical changes. As I drove through the city of Atlanta, I saw signs stating, "Silence is betrayal," and "South Asians 4 Black Lives," and "Black Lives Matter." Everyday people were taking to the streets to say they'd had enough. It nearly brings me to tears to remember it now.

The hopefulness of these moments, however, was also met with complexity and doubt. I couldn't help but wonder: *Have the protestors in this majority white, wealthy neighborhood discussed how racist housing policies have locked Black people out of their community for decades?*

I wondered, *For the white companies that are posting Black Lives Matter, do their boards and leadership teams reflect this sentiment? Do they organizationally value Black life?*

I kept asking myself, *Have these White pastors, who are suddenly speaking up about racism, done any work to consider how their traditions are steeped in exclusion and white racial superiority?*

I thought: *Yes, these leaders have great intentions, but I don't think they've done the work required to truly undermine systemic and pervasive racism; the root of the problem.*

Cracks, and more cracks, in the foundation.

A gap between what we think racism is, and what racism actually is.

Story #3

This third story is more personal. It recounts an experience I had with a former mentor, Stephen.[3] I share this story because I want to illuminate how a leader's good intentions can go awry in professional relationships, especially where racial, cultural, age, and power dynamics are at play.

I'd been involved in this new community for a few months. I was excited and humbled to participate. I knew I had a lot to offer, but as a creative, young person who preferred unconventional ways of working, I often struggled to find purposeful and autonomous work. This new opportunity seemed to offer a bit of both.

When I joined the organization, Stephen knew I was passionate about racial justice. I'd been leading anti-racism trainings and racial justice dialogues for a few years. I also had a blog in which I shared my thoughts on reconciliation, faith, and justice. I was finding my groove and my voice as an aspiring social entrepreneur. I sought out Stephen's mentorship because I wanted to learn the ropes of leading an enterprise of my own.

Even though I loved my work and was amped to belong to this new community, after a few months, multiple things started to feel a bit off.

Prior to joining this organization, I'd posted a blog that was critical of a different majority-white organization in the city. Much like what I'm writing about now, this group claimed to care about racial justice, but its team did not reflect this care; the entire team was white. From a public perspective, their "diversity work" was mere lip service and came from a desire to be relevant, not from a desire to dignify Black people and their stories. I wrote about this and shared it online.

Months later, after giving me an unrelated writing task as mentee homework, Stephen made a passing comment about how he didn't want me to write anything critical as I'd done before. He went on to describe how problematic my tone was, and he said something to the effect of, "You have to decide who you are going to be. If your tone is critical, you won't gain influence."

It took me a minute to even catch on to what he was saying. This all came out of left field.

Now, I want to pause here and give voice to what Stephen's intentions were in this moment. We don't always get to know what people's intentions are when they say or do something harmful, but since Stephen and I still know each other (and have discussed this story at length), I have the privilege of knowing what he was actually thinking.

When he was giving me this feedback, his thoughts were:

Bethaney is creative, talented, and ambitious. If she can learn from me over the next year or so, she will be well positioned to write books, lead organizations, and more. I want to set her up for success and give her access to platforms that will allow her message to spread.

Good intentions. Great intentions, even. But at the time, what I heard in our interaction was:

"Bethaney, don't tell the truth about racism and don't speak up in your authentic voice. If you do, you won't gain influence. Become like me, and I'll show you how to lead."

I was deeply hurt and offended. As an ambitious young woman in my early twenties, I was also impressionable. His opinion filled me with self-doubt. It was paralyzing. His comments, though well meaning, cut my authentic leadership off at the knees.

In the moment, he established a precedent that communicated to me: *Comfortable messaging for White people is more important than the truth of Black people's experiences.*

Said another way: *My comfort and buy-in as a White person is more important than your authentic voice.*

Said another way: *I am the expert in gaining influence, and my way is what's best. If you go about this your way, it won't work, and people won't respect you.*

Said another way: *Don't talk honestly about racism here.*

In this moment, Stephen not only criticized my authentic voice, he also silenced honest feedback about racism. I instantly felt I could never be direct and honest in this environment, because my belonging depended on my assimilation (*become like us*) and my submission (*follow, trust, and do not question*).

The ironic thing is I was the only Black person in the organization at the time.

If I wasn't "permitted" to be honest about racism, who would be? How would an all-white organization ever become more diverse if the people of color on the team couldn't be honest about their experiences within the organization? How would this organization ever change?

This was the first in a long line of trust-breaking moments for me. Even though Stephen had gone out of his way to connect with and mentor me, he was not yet equipped to lead me in an empowering way.

I know he had great intentions. Most of us do. But the impact of his comment in that moment, and other moments, sent me on a multiyear journey to find my voice all over again.

Cracks in the foundation.

Diversity isn't the problem; racism and white supremacy are the problem. And this problem impacts all of us: the person of color who's new to the team and searching for their voice, as well as the White person who means well but doesn't know how their good intentions might cause harm.[4]

WHAT IS RACISM, REALLY?

In an effort to understand racism, it's helpful to have a working understanding of race.

Race is a social construct. It's something people made up in order to sort and organize humans into groups.

Race has played different roles in society across time and place. For example, in ancient times, there was the "slave race" and the "free race." It had nothing to do with skin color; it was about class and socioeconomic status. In the United States, however, race (though tied to class) is mostly about skin color.

Race is unitary, which means the categories are singular and fixed. This often presents a challenge for biracial and multiracial people because they don't fit into society's racial boxes. Research consistently shows how people construct fixed ideas about what it means to be a "Black person," an "Asian person," and so on, and how humans use stereotypes to manage expectations of others based on appearance.

Race is about how you are perceived, not about who you actually are. As such, if you are perceived as a Black American, it doesn't matter that perhaps you were born in Nigeria, raised in Germany, and that English is your second language. Race is all about how other people see you.

Last, race is inherently hierarchical. This is where an understanding of racism and white supremacy begin to unfold.

THE METAPHORICAL, AND HIERARCHICAL, LADDER

Imagine a hierarchy as people on a ladder. There is someone higher up on the ladder and someone lower on the ladder. If you are higher on the ladder, you're considered more valuable, more attractive, more trustworthy, and so on. If you are lower on the ladder, you're considered less valuable, less attractive, and less trustworthy.

In the United States, the racial hierarchy places White people, as well as White cultural norms and practices, at the top of the ladder. This same hierarchy places Black people, and thus Black cultural norms and practices, at the bottom of the ladder. This hierarchy has existed for centuries and has been reinforced through policies, economics, and institutional practices throughout history.

In terms of how the hierarchy functions, the cultural norms piece matters a lot.

Here's why: If you are a Black person who adopts white cultural norms, you move up the ladder. If you are an Asian person who adopts white cultural norms, you move up the ladder. If you are a Latino who adopts white cultural norms, you move up the ladder. However, if you are a person from any racial category and you adopt black cultural norms or practices associated with blackness, you move down the ladder.

What does it mean to move up the ladder? It means society views you as more valuable, more "normal," more trustworthy, more honest, more human, superior, and so on.

What does it mean to move down the ladder? It means society views you as less valuable, less "normal," less trust-worthy, less honest, less human, inferior, and so on.

When racial hierarchy is layered on top of the many identity hierarchies prevalent in culture (gender, age, sexual orientation, class, educational attainment, ability, etc.), we discover how people's unique combination of identity markers makes them more or less valuable in the eyes of society as a whole.

Intersectionality

Intersectionality is a term coined by Dr. Kimberle Crenshaw. In simple terms, intersectionality refers to the way identities exist at various intersections of identity markers. Each person carries a race, a gender identity, a nationality, a degree of educational attainment, and so on. As such, based on a unique combination of markers, we experience marginalization differently. The experience of oppression is compounded for those whose identity intersections are devalued in United States culture and society.

Here is a chart breaking down various identity markers and how they have been ranked throughout history in the United States.

Identity Markers	Higher on the Ladder	Lower on the Ladder
Economic Status	Wealthy	Poor
Educational Attainment	More degrees	No degrees
Ability	Able	Disabled
Language	Standard American English	English as a Second Language or Various Vernaculars of English
Gender Identity	Man	Woman
Race	White	Black

Each of these identity markers exists on its own spectrum and as part of its own hierarchy. While this book focuses on diversity gaps related to race and racism, you will likely find these additional hierarchies at play in your organizational context as well. When closing diversity gaps in reference to more than one identity marker, your challenge is to address the *compounded* marginalization experienced by people whose identity intersections are devalued in US society and within your organization.

If you are higher up on the ladder, you tend to be paid the most, you have the most positional authority or power, and you get to make the most decisions or make decisions impacting the most people. When the police or other authority figures interact with you, your first reaction isn't one of valid fear. Instead, you're given the benefit of the doubt. When you apply for a loan, your race does not count against you. You are generally trusted to speak, to curate, to lead, and to give advice. When you walk into a room, more often than not you can rest assured you belong there. If you are in a place of business and you ask to speak to the person in charge, you are likely to be met by someone who looks like you. When you go to your place of worship, you're likely to see people who look like you at the microphone. When you read history books, the most prominent figures and stories are about people who share your race. When you purchase books for children, most characters look like you. When you pause to consider who has had the most access to writing laws and defining what it means to be an American citizen, again, you're in the company of people cut from a similar racial cloth as you.

If this is your experience, you're probably at the top of the ladder—either because you're White (and male) or because you've worked really hard to adapt to and embody the norms that white culture values most.

This is white supremacy in the organizational context: an environment where white cultural values and norms are in the center of how we lead and how organizations operate.

You're at the top of the ladder, not because you're more important than or superior to other people, but because your personal origin story—where you were born and the body you were born into—is located within a broader historical and social context that has routinely advantaged White bodies, while simultaneously creating barriers for Black bodies, Indigenous bodies, Asian bodies, and other bodies of color for centuries.

In many ways, this is an oversimplification intended to illustrate a point about racial advantage and white privilege. However, we could construct similar nuanced analyses based on gender, socioeconomic status, ability, and more. I point you to the section above where we discuss intersectionality.

Ultimately:

> **Racism** is a system of advantage and disadvantage based on race; "advantage" for those higher up on the ladder and "disadvantage" for those lower on the ladder.

> **Racism** is not only reflected in the mean things "bad people" say and do.

> **Racism** is not all race-related prejudice and discrimination.

In leading racial justice education workshops, I've found many of us conflate racism with other forms of identity-based discrimination. We fail to acknowledge how *stereotyping* is different from *prejudice*, which are both different from *discrimination*, which is different from *ethnocentrism*. This isn't about semantics. It is important for you to understand. When we call everything racism, it's another way of calling nothing racism. Sometimes, this debate about what racism is and isn't is used as a stalling tactic to keep us from discussing the problem at hand: a system of advantage and disadvantage based on race.

• • ● ● • •

When we call everything racism, it's another way of calling nothing racism.

• • ● ● • •

Addressing racism requires specificity about racism.

Sometimes racism is fueled by evil intentions. More often than not, however, it's fueled by an unintentional, and sometimes invisible, compliance with the "old way" things have been done.

To better understand this "old way," one must also understand white supremacy.[5]

WHITE SUPREMACY CULTURE

Earlier, when I referenced adopting "white cultural norms," you may have thought to yourself, *What norms?* Honestly, there are many. Not only do White people descend from different nations, each with their own unique histories and stories, but white culture in the United States is also diverse in values, perspectives, accents, and more. This diversity, like all diversity, is a gift.

When I reference white cultural norms, I'm specifically referring to what many scholars have defined as "white supremacy culture." Frances Lee Ansley describes white supremacy as "a political, economic, and cultural system in which white people overwhelmingly control power and material resources." In this cultural system, "conscious and unconscious ideas of white superiority and entitlement are widespread, and relations of white dominance and nonwhite subordination are daily reenacted across a broad array of institutions and social settings."[6]

To sit with this definition of white supremacy means to see reality playing out in the United States daily:

A values-driven, "do-good" organization where the entire executive leadership team and the majority of the board of directors are all White people. It's likely this team has a stated value for diversity on their website. It's also likely they've "tried" hiring people of color in the past but it "just didn't work out." This organization feels really good about their work. They hustle to export their world-changing ideas around the globe. They say all the right things, post the right hashtags, and are skilled at "amplifying melanated voices" on public platforms when the cultural moment demands it. But, at the end of the day—despite all their posturing, apologizing, reading, and podcast-listening—power and resources remain firmly in their grasp.

White supremacy is a *culture*. And like every culture, it is upheld and reinforced by a set of values, stories, symbols, norms, and practices. It's embedded in how we behave.

The tricky thing about culture is this: while we can choose values for ourselves, many values are chosen for us by the culture in which we live. These values remain underneath the surface of how we think, how we make decisions, how we create organizations, to whom we allow ourselves to be accountable, and most certainly how we lead. These values also shape our personal and organizational origin stories.

Authors and social justice facilitators Tema Okun and Kenneth Jones, in the creation of their resource, *Dismantling Racism: A Workbook for Social Change Groups*,[7] highlight thirteen values of white supremacy culture. Each value is an invitation for you to 1) acknowledge them within yourself, and 2) acknowledge them within your organization.

- Perfectionism
- Sense of Urgency
- Defensiveness
- Quantity over Quality
- Worship of the Written Word
- Paternalism
- Either/Or Thinking
- Power Hoarding
- Fear of Open Conflict
- Individualism
- Progress Is Bigger, More
- Objectivity
- Right to Comfort

Here are ways these values play out in organizations, both in general and as it relates to efforts to build racially diverse teams in dignifying ways.

#1. Perfectionism—
"If we're going to do this, it has to be perfect."

Making mistakes causes shame; leaders are reluctant to speak up about racial injustice because they fear doing and saying the wrong thing.

#2. Sense of Urgency—"The moment is now!"

Building inclusive teams, creating relationships of mutuality, building trust, unlearning bias, and so on—all this work takes time. However, because of the orientation toward fast and measurable results, it is tempting to settle with short-term Band-Aids over long-term change. This value also speaks to the ways "hustle" and "busyness" define much of organizational life.

#3. Defensiveness—
"This is the way we've always done it, and I know it works."

A great deal of effort goes into protecting the status quo. When threats to the status quo arise, either in the form of new thinking or new people, they are met with discomfort, hostility, and, ultimately, rejection.

#4. Quantity over Quality—
"What gets measured gets managed."

More value is placed on what can be measured than on what is important, yet unmeasurable. This value is always asking, "How many?" instead of asking, "How well?" or "How effective?" or "How valuable?"

#5. Worship of the Written Word— "Yes, but the rules say . . ."

Stories, ideas, and beliefs in written form are deemed truer and more valuable than stories, ideas, and beliefs transmitted in other ways. For example, people are more likely to take what I'm saying seriously because I've "authored a book," even though there may be people in your organization or on your team who have been sharing similar ideas with you in real life.

#6. Paternalism— "I know what's best, and my way is for the greater good."

Leaders and powerholders believe they are entitled to make decisions for other people, and believe their ideas are universally applicable. Arrogance, control, and manipulation are masked as "visionary leadership." The language of "family" is used to coerce and enforce the submission of others.

#7. Either/Or Thinking—"There is no gray area on this."

This one is as simple as it sounds. Reality exists as a binary: either/or, good/bad, right/wrong, with us/against us. These cultures tend to create a strong insider/outsider mentality, where disagreement or any form of divergence means you can't belong.

#8. Power Hoarding—
"I'm the only one who can take this where it needs to go."

Even though leaders who are hoarding power can rarely see or admit it, deep down they believe power is limited. They believe sharing power will be too costly. When their sense of control is threatened, these leaders write off new people and new ideas as inexperienced or ill-informed. These leaders cannot imagine a future in which they are not "the leader."

#9. Fear of Open Conflict—
"I would listen to their feedback if they said it more politely."

In cultures where people fear open conflict, honest dialogue about identity, race, and diversity is nearly impossible. Extreme value is placed on "being nice" and "being polite." This is problematic, because there is no "right way" to handle conflict. In white supremacy culture, open conflict is a nonstarter.

#10. Individualism—"There can only be one winner."

When individualism is a value, organizations focus on individual achievement over teamwork. They also foster a culture of competition over a culture of collaboration. Even if one's internal team works collaboratively, in white supremacy culture, other organizations in a similar industry are viewed as a threat to be disregarded, invalidated, or destroyed.

#11. Progress Is Bigger, More—
"If you're not growing, you're dying."

This value is at work when organizations focus on expanding their geographical footprint rather than creatively and more deeply building community. Scaling and growth are always celebrated, while little thought is given to purposefully staying small and serving a few people really well. There is a high value placed on more people, more money, more territory, and more programs. This paradigm ignores the fact that when endless growth of cells happens in our bodies, it's called cancer.

#12. Objectivity—
"I have a logical, balanced perspective here."

All perspectives are informed by a specific cultural lens. However, people who adopt this value of objectivity believe their perspective is normal and universal, rather than cultural. They downplay the role of social location and emotions in their decision making. When this value is at work, leaders struggle to appreciate multiple and diverse ways of knowing and understanding the world.

#13. Right to Comfort—
"If you're going to talk about race, let me (the person who has never experienced racism) tell you the best way to do that."

When diversity programs and trainings prioritize the comfort of those in power, it rarely moves the needle for change.

Discomfort is where all growth and learning begin. However, if you believe you're entitled to comfort at all times, then you will never be in a situation where diversity, inclusion, or liberation from oppressive systems are possible.

It's important to pause now and take inventory. Read the list below and check off the values of white supremacy culture you have observed in yourself, as well as the ones you've observed in your organization.

Value	Within Myself	Within My Organization
Perfectionism		
Sense of Urgency		
Defensiveness		
Quantity over Quality		
Worship of the Written Word		
Paternalism		
Either/Or Thinking		
Power Hoarding		
Fear of Open Conflict		
Individualism		
Progress Is Bigger, More		
Objectivity		
Right to Comfort		

For the sake of transparency, here's what my grid looks like at the time of this writing:

Value	Within Myself	Within My Organization
Perfectionism	x	
Sense of Urgency	x	x
Defensiveness	x	x
Quantity over Quality	x	x
Worship of the Written Word	x	
Paternalism	x	x
Either/Or Thinking		x
Power Hoarding		x
Fear of Open Conflict	x	
Individualism	x	x
Progress Is Bigger, More		x
Objectivity		x
Right to Comfort		x

Do you have to be racially white to ascribe to the culture of white supremacy?

Nope.

This is the culture we all live in. It's also the defining culture of the vast majority of mainstream leadership and organizational life. To be a successful and influential leader in today's world, we are taught, implicitly and explicitly, to embody the values above. As such, people from a variety of racial and ethnic backgrounds adopt these values.

● ● ●

CONNECTING THE DOTS

Let's revisit the three stories I shared earlier to connect the dots between these stories and the prevalence of racism and white supremacy in everyday leadership and organizational experiences. By understanding these systemic cultural dynamics, you will be better equipped to disrupt them in yourself and your organization.

Story #1:
The Conference on Unity Created by a Majority White Organization

In this story, the three values of white supremacy culture were: quantity over quality, paternalism, and power hoarding.

Quantity over Quality. There were at least five non-White racial-justice thought leaders in the speaker lineup for this event. When looking at the website, they made up a large percentage of the presenters. However, their perspectives and contributions were given the least overall stage time. As an attendee, I left having heard extensively from White men, and minimally from any other perspective. From what I could tell, the quantity of non-White faces in the speaker lineup meant more to the conference organizers than creating space for the quality, or substance, of what the non-White leaders could have shared if allotted more time and space to do so.

Paternalism. Even though the conference planning team had almost no racial and ethnic diversity, these leaders still felt entitled to host an event on cross-cultural and racial unity. One of the functions of paternalism in white supremacy culture is it leads to White people, and most often White men, acting as though they are the final authority or the guiding expert on every topic—even topics with which they have zero firsthand experience: for example, with systemic racism.

Power Hoarding. The voices and perspectives of White musicians, speakers, authors, and entrepreneurs took up most of the space during this event on racial unity. The people who held the mic had the power and authority to shape the experience of attendees. By concentrating this influential power in the hands of White people, it reinforced the narrative that white voices, perspectives, and leadership ideas are more important than others.

Story #2:
#BlackLivesMatter, but Not in Our Neighborhoods or on Our Teams

Worship of the Written Word. The most obvious way this value emerged during the 2020 racial uprising was in how countless organizations and companies created statements about their "commitment to diversity." They posted stories online, sent multiple email campaigns, and even updated their website landing pages to affirm #BlackLivesMatter. Even though I loved seeing this regular affirmation of Black dignity, I wondered how many of these teams felt that writing something was enough. It's tempting to believe that if something is written down, its authoritative. However, just because it's written down and well designed doesn't mean it's a felt reality in these contexts.

Sense of Urgency. One of the most challenging aspects of pursuing racial justice in society these days is getting the pacing right. What does it look like to advocate for change in the heat of the moment, while also preparing for long-term engagement? Even though I was thrilled to see so many people from all racial and ethnic backgrounds engaged in advocacy and protest, I wondered: *Are they on track to burn out? Is the busyness and frantic energy of this season sustainable?* I understand wanting to fix the problem of racism overnight; I've longed for it. But the notion that one can wake up to the reality of racism one week, and completely understand, dismantle, and then teach others how to move through it next week, is very unrealistic. You can't move with urgency forever. You have to slow down long enough to increase awareness, analyze what is seen, and then move toward actions in ways that are authentic and integrated.

Story #3:
I Want You on My Team, but Check Your Voice and Perspective at the Door

Objectivity (and Paternalism). One of the trickiest aspects of white supremacy culture is that as the values are folded in together, they serve to ultimately reinforce white supremacy itself—in other words, a culture wherein White people maintain control of power and material resources. In the case of objectivity, leaders who are White believe their perspectives to be linear, logical, and correct in most every situation. They rarely question this. They also believe these perspectives to be culturally neutral and free of emotion. Combining a belief in objectivity with paternalism creates a situation in which White people feel entitled to critique and diminish the leadership habits, practices, and perspectives of other cultures.

When Stephen told me how to best communicate about racism—a phenomenon he'd read about but never experienced—he believed his perspective was objectively true and that he was entitled to tell me how to best use my voice.

Because he was my mentor, there was a power differential we each informally agreed to when I accepted his guidance in my life. The nature of this relationship (mentor–mentee) gave Stephen the positional authority to give me direction and correction. But his posture in this scenario lacked curiosity and humility; it was also culturally insensitive.

Objectivity lends itself to believing in cultural neutrality. But his comments were not neutral. They were highly informed by his experiences as a White man and organizational leader in the United States. This cultural insensitivity is not only relevant to conversations on racism. **There are cultural implications to every aspect of organizational leadership**, including raising money, creating content, building a team, designing events, and purchasing buildings. It is all culturally informed. Objectivity is a myth.

Either/Or Thinking. Why were there only two options? Why couldn't it be possible for me to speak honestly about racism on my blog *and* for me to speak optimistically on the part of the organization? Why did I have to choose one tone or the other? Both were true. But for Stephen, from my perspective, it was as if only one tone was acceptable, right, and good. If I used a tone of criticism and analysis, I was out. If I used a tone of ease and comfort (for White folks), I was in.

I chose the latter to stay involved in the organization. This is a decision people of color make all the time and at great personal, emotional, and mental cost. Racial, ethnic, and cultural diversity cannot emerge and thrive in situations where we cannot hold multiple, complex realities at one time.

Defensiveness. Last, but not least: Stephen exhibited defensiveness by suggesting that my honest tone, which he read as critical, nonconstructive, and untrustworthy, was a threat to the status quo of what it means to lead and gain influence in today's world. On the one hand, maybe he was right. Historically, White people have not enjoyed honest and direct communication about racism. And yet, the irony remains: Is it possible to build a racially diverse, culturally inclusive, creative, and impactful team if one's knee-jerk posture is to defend the status quo, silence uncomfortable voices, and resist the disruption of change?

WHERE DO WE GO FROM HERE?

The key insight of this chapter is this: Your team's lack of diversity is not the root problem; racism and white supremacy are the root problems.

Racism is a system of advantage and disadvantage based on race. Within this system, White people not only hold the most power and control, they also experience the greatest degree of entitlement to that power and control. These dynamics are difficult, though not impossible, to change.

To begin the process of change, you have to revisit your origin stories—both personally and organizationally. You have to take an honest look at how underrepresented racial and ethnic minorities experience your organization. What is the felt and honest impact of your leadership on the people of color who work for you? You also have to explore how your traditional diversity programming is or is not creating a dignifying culture where all people can truly thrive.

In the next chapter, I amplify the voices of various people of color (Black people, Indigenous people, multiracial people, Asian people, Latino/a people, etc.) who shared with me their thoughts on what it takes to confront racism and white supremacy in organizations. I specifically asked each of these leaders, "If you could tell your White or majority culture peers one thing without fear of being misunderstood or silenced, what would you say?"

As you listen to these community voices, my encouragement to you is to lean in, listen well, and let them impact you as they have powerfully impacted me. As a leader who aspires to create a culture where authentic racial and ethnic diversity can flourish, your task is to listen and learn from those who have been negatively impacted by racism and white supremacy. Those who have experienced the problem have the keenest insights on how to solve the problem.

Read, listen, and believe their stories.

IMPACT OVER INTENTIONS

- *Insight:* The impact of your organizational culture on people of color is more important than your good intentions.

- *Action:* Prioritize hearing, believing, and following people of color.

AMPLIFYING
MARGINALIZED VOICES

Over the next few pages, we are going to dive into a collection of community voices. In my research, I interviewed Black people, Indigenous people, multiracial people, and people of color (BIPOC) to better understand their experiences navigating predominately white institutions.

This is important for a few reasons.

First, your efforts to create a diverse organization will affect real people. Real humans with real stories, identities, limitations, hopes, career aspirations, and fears. While you may bring a world of good intentions to your efforts to increase racial and ethnic diversity in your organization, if your efforts cause repeated or unintended harm, the burden of responsibility is on *you* to change course. Listening to these often silenced or marginalized perspectives is a step toward addressing the impact "increasing diversity" can have on BIPOC.

The second reason to amplify these perspectives is because the people who experience a problem are the people who should drive its solution. People of color often experience the harmful weight of racism and white supremacy culture. Therefore, their leadership is essential in addressing this form of oppression in the organizational context.

THE NARRATIVE BATTLE

One of the challenges you may encounter as you begin amplifying historically marginalized perspectives is the narrative battle. The narrative battle is what happens when an organization's origin story collides with the counternarratives of those who've been historically excluded. This battle, depicted in the stories below, is nothing short of ferocious. It's a fight from which few people leave unaffected, but the greatest harm is often inflicted on leaders of color who choose to speak out.

· · ● · ● · ·

One of the challenges
you may encounter as you
begin amplifying historically
marginalized perspectives
is the narrative battle.

· · ● · ● · ·

PROTECTING THE ORIGIN STORY

One of the pillars of maintaining the racial hierarchy within organizations, and in society at large, is the policing of stories. People go to great lengths to maintain strict, though often informal, boundaries around which stories get told and which stories get silenced.

Many organizations have an origin story. This story comprises narratives in which the founder, or the founding community, is uplifted as the hero. These stories are told over and over again as a way to establish culture. These stories also remind an organization of who they are and what they are about. These stories are fiercely protected.

Here are a few general examples.

- "We were a group of friends passionate about changing the world. We flew to another country, began volunteering, and felt like the work could be done better. So, we came back home, rallied a community of supporters, and we started [x] nonprofit. We've been working in communities all over the world ever since."

- "We were sitting around a dinner table, and we got an idea. Everyone around the table agreed it was awesome. We built a website overnight, and the project exploded. We were picked up by a national news outlet, and our story took off. We began teaching others how to do what we were doing. This was the beginning of our work. Our city and the world are better because of it."

- "Our hearts were broken over an international crisis. We began asking, what can we do in our part of the world to solve this problem? We've always wanted our lives to be about impacting the most marginalized. We created a business model, raised the funds, and have been slowly but surely moving the needle on this issue for more than two decades."

Sound familiar?

More often than not, these stories begin with a homogenous group of people solving a "problem" in total isolation from those impacted by the problem. There is rarely, if any, critical analysis where leaders ask themselves hard but important questions, such as:

"Has anyone tried solving this problem before?"

"How are people within this community already trying to solve this problem?"

"Why do I think my solution is the best option?"

"Am I being paternalistic? Do I want to be the hero?"

"Am I experiencing true success in this work, or is this actually my privilege on display?"

"What roles have racism and white supremacy played in creating this problem I'm trying to solve?"

"What is my responsibility to address racism and white supremacy before bringing my idea to life?"

Taking it one layer deeper, the people who create and tell these stories have a vested interest in the stories never being challenged. The line of thinking is: "I have great intentions and great ideas. Hundreds, if not thousands, of people have been positively impacted by my leadership. I am a good person and a good leader. I deserve to be in charge, and I'm entitled to do this work in the world."

However, over time, as people from socially marginalized groups begin to raise an eyebrow of suspicion or express a counternarrative to the origin story, it fundamentally threatens the status quo. It threatens who leaders believe themselves to be. It exposes the cracks in the foundation. In a very real way, counternarratives threaten the job security of the leader and the existence of the organization as a whole.

WHEN ORIGIN STORIES AND
COUNTERNARRATIVES COLLIDE

On a national level, you've probably seen this play out in our collective reckoning with police brutality. One group of US citizens calls for the abolition of the police, while a different group of US citizens calls for the protection of the police. How can we arrive at two entirely different responses?

One cultural origin story says, "The policing establishment was created to protect and serve us, and we need them."

There's also the counternarrative, largely from marginalized communities of color, and it says, "The policing establishment was created to hunt and kill us, and it has to stop."

This is a narrative battle. We arrive at different responses based on our social location, our origin story, and the stories we believe about ourselves, others, and the world.

On an organizational level, a narrative battle will often occur between a majority white organization and a woman of color who joins the team.

The organization's priority is to tell and protect its origin story at all costs. When a woman of color joins the organization, she tends to fit in as long as she upholds the story. However, once she begins to voice a counternarrative, or when she leads in ways the organization finds threatening, organizational forces push the woman of color out. She moves on, because she's fired or because the environment becomes so toxic she has to leave for the sake of her mental and emotional health.

In March 2018, the Centre for Community Organizations (COCo) published an infographic depicting the journey of women of color in the workplace.[1] The woman of color enters the organization and moves through four phases: honeymoon, reality, response, and retaliation. At each phase, the white leadership of the organization behaves toward the woman in a particular way.

> **Honeymoon Phase:** The woman of color feels excited, energized, and happy to be on the team. The white leadership treats her as a tokenized hire: "We've started to check our diversity box!"

> **Reality Phase:** The woman of color begins to express her counternarrative. She voices concerns about issues in the organization; she tries to work within the organization's structures; and she pushes for the organization to do something about the issues at hand. In this phase, harmful pressures of the white dominant culture become apparent, often through microaggressions (e.g., regularly commenting on the woman of color's appearance) or through expecting the woman of color to address internal organizational race issues without giving her the authority or pay to do so.

> **Response Phase:** The white leadership denies racism and blames or ignores the woman of color. The woman of color is held responsible for fixing the problem, and she is often pitted against other

people of color in the organization by way of comparison: "Why can't you be more like [insert other racial minority here]? [He or she] is happy and loves being here!"

Retaliation Phase: The organization targets and attacks. The woman of color is deemed a poor "cultural fit," or the conflict is chalked up to a communication problem.

One of the most illuminating aspects of the research conducted by COCo is how people perceive why underrepresented racial minorities leave the organization. While nearly 30 percent of the people of color surveyed by COCo said they left a job due to an "unwelcoming racial environment," White respondents often gave different reasons, perceiving that their non-White peers left because they found a better job or because they wanted more family time.[2] The COCo report states, "Overall, white respondents underestimated how many people of color were leaving their jobs because of discrimination by 15 percent."[3]

You may think people of color are leaving your organization for reasons unrelated to racial dynamics, when research shows many people of color move on specifically because of them.[4]

The narrative battle between the origin stories of the majority culture and the counternarratives of the marginalized is a persistent challenge in our efforts to create racial and ethnically diverse organizations.

Assessing the Harm

When origin stories and counternarratives collide, it typically causes more harm to the carrier of the counternarrative than it does to the maintainers of the origin story.

The carrier of the counternarrative endures varying degrees of racial trauma, as well as the accompanying emotional and psychological labor required to navigate and heal from it.

The maintainers of the origin story typically go on, business as usual, believing they are justified in the calls they make to protect the organization and its work.

Racism and white supremacy march onward seemingly unphased. People of color continue to be silenced and endure trauma and marginalization.

I have spent years suppressing the counternarratives I see and feel. As a Black woman who has worked in many predominately white institutions, suppressing the truth of my perspective became second nature for a variety of reasons.

Sometimes the counternarrative was explicitly silenced, as was the case when it felt like Stephen (see chapter one) effectively told me not to speak honestly and directly about racism. Or in other instances when I was "too young," "too inexperienced," or "too lacking in expertise" for my perspective on racial dynamics to be valid.

I've also silenced my own counternarratives because I didn't want to experience the slow but sure rejection I'd watched other women of color in my workplace experience. I've silenced my counternarratives to keep my job because I needed the money, to make sure White people felt comfortable in my presence, and to avoid losing a sense of exceptionalism and belonging.

Over time, this silencing gets lodged in one's body. The grief and pain of it all demands attention. For me, at the time of this writing, I'm in a season of learning how to no longer suppress my counternarratives, because doing so has created physical and mental health challenges for me.

In a very real way, when counternarratives from the racial and ethnic margins of an organization collide with White people's origin stories, the result is usually subjugation, termination, minimalization, and even death for Black people, Indigenous people, and various peoples of color.

I'm describing this dynamic in detail because I want you to have a robust, emotional, and textured perspective on what it *really* looks like to center and amplify the voices of historically marginalized racial and ethnic communities.

• • ● • •

This is not something we do to be cute, to check a box, or to be relevant.

• • ● • •

To truly center and amplify perspectives from the margins is to fundamentally reorient everything *you* believe to be true about who *you* are, what *you* do, and how *you* lead.

Additionally, when we center and amplify perspectives from the margins, we discover new antidotes to racism and white supremacy culture. The way forward will not be charted by those who've benefited from the oppressive structures of the past. The way forward will be paved by the stories, creativity, ingenuity, and delightful engagement of those who have historically been on the margins. One way to resolve the narrative battle is to continually practice active listening and allow uncomfortable perspectives to emerge and transform the organization.

LISTENING TO MARGINALIZED VOICES

Here are ten stories from people of color whose perspectives illuminate the impact majority white organizational cultures can have on underrepresented racial minorities. I pulled from a diverse cross section of racial and ethnic identities and industries. Names have been removed to protect their identities.

As you read, silence the outside world and let these stories be at the front and center of your heart, mind, and imagination. Honor these people with belief. It is not enough to amplify BIPOC stories; you must also believe them. More important, in time, you must change how you lead in light of what you hear and learn.

Black woman: After spending eleven years in corporate marketing, this interviewee left to work for an international development nonprofit. Below is her description of going to work each day as the only Black person on her corporate team.

I spent a lot of time compartmentalizing just to exist. I spent years putting walls around myself so I could just be. I would think to myself, *I know that all they want me to do is come in and smile and be a cultural fit.* That's literally all I tried to do. I would literally be clenching, clenching, clenching all the time. Smiling. Just trying to get by. I was the only Black person in a sea of White folks. Older White folks who had been around a long time certainly couldn't understand an environment where a Black woman could be competent, self-assured, and not ask for their opinion.

Taiwanese American man: This interviewee worked in corporate engineering and was one of the few non-White people in his firm.

Me: Do you think you can experience belonging in this environment?

As a Taiwanese American man, I have aspects of both Eastern and Western cultures. It's tricky to figure out what part of me is assimilating into this culture, and what part of me is just being part of this culture. I don't have to code switch that often, and I feel like I can bring up culture in ways that feel appropriate when I need to.

Me: If there was one thing you could tell your majority culture peers without fear of being misunderstood or silenced, what would you say?

The one thing that comes to mind is the hardest for me to explain. I would say . . . I'm always subconsciously fighting against saving face at work. The Asian side of me is more accustomed to saving face at work. But that's not an accepted Western business practice. So, I do some things one way, but it would be more acceptable or be perceived as more honest or more status quo if I do it another way.

If I could explain that to others, I would.

Black woman: This woman works for a national, faith-based nonprofit. In many of her roles, she was the only Black person on her team. Over time, she's worked to shift her role within the organization to work with more Black people and other underrepresented racial minorities.

Me: If you could tell your White peers one thing without fear of being misunderstood or silenced, what would it be?

You will never understand the real cost of being in my body within this white space. Recognize there is a cost. A holistic cost. For you, you just have to show up to work each day. But for us non-White people, we have to show up to work and deal with your microaggressions, deal with creating strategy for all people of color, and do our jobs excellently, because we know we're being judged harsher. We end up saying yes to doing more work, because we're often the only people of color.

It piles so high to the point where it has a holistic cost on my emotional, psychological, and physical well-being. White folks cannot understand this cost. Yes, I have agency and, yes, I'm learning to make different decisions. But the cost is real, and you are a part of that cost. I don't want you to feel sorry for me. But you need to do something different in your very being in order to change who we are as an organization and how we function. Because I'm human.

Me: Is there anything else on your mind you want to share?

The question most White folks start to ask is, "Okay, what do I do?" And the truth is, we do need them to do things. There are legitimate things to do. Like, you need to change your behavior. You need to implement new policies. You need to hire certain people. You need to go to specific places. And at the end of the day, it's also a transformation of being that we're asking for.

Racism is pervasive and it's everywhere. In our very beings, our very bodies. We're talking about bodies. And so, as you are doing, we hope that what you are doing informs your being. What does your being actually look like? Also know that there are tons of people out there who do this work and whom you can observe as they are being anti-racist. Learning from them could be helpful.

Afro-Latina woman: This interviewee worked in corporate marketing and advertising before leaving to start her own consultancy.

Me: If you could tell your majority culture peers one thing without fear of being misunderstood or silenced, what would it be?

Everybody makes mistakes. It's all about how you react when you realize you've made a mistake. It's all about having the humility to be vocal about it and say, "I'm sorry."

It's important to let go of egos and to go back and really try to understand what you did wrong—not necessarily putting the burden on the people you've harmed to explain it to you, unless they are open to that. But know that we are all making mistakes. Language is evolving, and the space is evolving, so we're all learning and unlearning. We're all on a journey, and we're all figuring it out. I understand the hesitation, but we're all going through that. Don't let the fear of saying the wrong thing keep you from doing the right thing.

Black man: This interviewee is a corporate consultant. He also leads his company's internal diversity and inclusion work. Below, he tells a story about discussing the performance reviews of his Black colleagues with his company president, who is White.

[My boss] and I were talking about examples of some Black employees that were in sales positions; they just weren't as successful as their counterparts. The leadership kind of chalked it up to the possibility that maybe sales wasn't something that these Black employees were very passionate about. I explained to him, you know, these Black employees were going into rooms where the people they were selling to were predominately White men and White women. If you go into the room as a White male, you're comfortable. You're speaking to your peers and speaking the same language. So, you're more comfortable. But if I go into the room as a Black male and I'm the only Black male at the table, there's a different dynamic in the room. I have to be mindful of how I talk, how I dress. Because I'm not only managing my unconscious biases, I'm managing all the biases of the people in the room as well. And I'm trying to create a sales "Aha" moment for them. It's a different dynamic than for my White peers, and it's a lot.

Me: What is it like being a racial minority in your work context?

There's an emotional tax when it comes to being a minority, and that's across the board. Sometimes Black employees and other minorities don't want to go out to client gatherings after work. We've spent so much time not necessarily being authentic because our authentic selves might not be embraced. At the end of the day, we're tired. We've been acting like somebody else all day. We just want to go home and be ourselves.

Me: How do you manage the emotional part of it? The emotional tax and emotional labor piece?

In my first few years in this space, coming out of college, I was twenty-two and working with clients all over the company and all over the country. I distinctly remember one of my clients having a very conservative culture. I had this assumption that they'd be racist, so I did my best to look older, to look more mature. I would wear a blazer, wear my glasses, I would grow out my facial hair, doing whatever I could to look like the people I was working with and to look older. I remember being so tired and so drained by four o'clock. On my lunch breaks, I would go back to my hotel to take a nap, because I was just so tired.

It eventually got to the point where I had to have a conversation with myself and that client. I had to ask, "Am I bringing value to this workplace?"

Yes.

"Is there anything I can improve?"

Yes, here are a few things.

"Are you happy with my performance?"

Yes, absolutely.

So, if I'm adding value and being productive, then it shouldn't matter how I look or how I talk. I shouldn't have to do all that extra work. I'm bringing value.

So, I had to have this conversation with myself, and then I slowly started to relax.

To reduce that emotional tax, remember: You are valuable. You are a high performer.

Me: If there was one thing you could tell your White or majority culture peers without fear of being misunderstood or silenced, what would it be?

To understand. To listen without wanting to respond, but to truly understand and empathize. We won't be able to make the progress we need without our White peers being allies and advocates for the change.

Me: Is there anything else you want me to know?

There is a lot of deep work that needs to be done when it comes to understanding unconscious bias. A quick training and seminar are not going to change your behavior. Those things are only one touchpoint. You can put up a commitment to diversity and start some employee resource groups and appear to be making a change. But until systemic behaviors change, you won't have sustained progress.

Biracial woman (Chinese and White American): This interviewee worked for a large healthcare nonprofit. Members of her team were mostly Black/African American women, but the organization as a whole was predominately white.

Me: What is the biggest diversity gap you see in your organization?

The biggest gap I see is when people view certain personality traits, ones that don't line up with majority culture or white cultural traits, as "less than" because they don't fit that mold. Assuming that, because they aren't wearing that coat of armor, they lack intelligence or aren't capable. I don't think anyone would admit that out loud, but I think women experience this, too. You have to play the game to get ahead, and I wish that we could celebrate all the characteristics that are natural to people. Otherwise, women and people of color have to overcompensate for who they are. And it's really exhausting and difficult. When you're putting that much effort into your daily work, it's automatically going to be more difficult for you to succeed in the same ways.

Me: If there was one thing you could tell your majority culture or White peers without fear of being misunderstood or silenced, what would it be?

I would say two things. People spend so much time thinking they do things the best way and trying to get others to do things their way. But it's okay that we don't all do things the same way.

Also, colorblind isn't the goal. It's not the goal. People's differences are good.

Black woman: This interviewee works for an international, poverty-relief nonprofit. The comments below were general thoughts she shared when asked if there was anything else on her mind related to race, diversity, and her organization.

What makes me feel super gross is the power dynamic around how we promote our work. It's almost exclusively Black and Brown faces used in the ways we tell stories. We are extremely extractive in our storytelling. But there are these words we use to describe ourselves as an organization, words like *social justice*. Words like *equality*. But what we don't want to do is the self-examination that is required to put people in power who don't currently have it.

Internally, while we have people of color, or diversity, in our staff members, they have absolutely no opportunity for growth at all. There are folks who have been in this building for fifteen years and have never gotten a promotion and have never gotten a raise. It's an overarching challenge. As soon as we hire diverse candidates, they are literally hemorrhaging out of the back door, because the experience they are having here is so poor. They don't feel supported. They have this existence where it's like, "Oh, you're novel! Oh, goodness, we brought in this diverse person! Oh, wow, thank you for coming! We're so excited; we want to hear what you have to say." And then they say it. And then there is this super-hostile, implicit bias they have to live through. They either leave or they're no longer a "cultural fit."

On top of everything, there's also the lack of transparency from the leadership about all of this.

Latina, biracial woman: This interviewee held a director-level position in an education nonprofit. The conversation below picks up with her describing a communication dynamic as a Latina manager in her organization.

I've told my team that they can handle me when I'm happy. They can handle me when I'm sad, but they can't handle me when I'm angry. So, I know that there are certain emotions that I can't exhibit. Like, if I am angry, I know that it's going to be on my face. And then I've got to talk about it. And sometimes I just want to be angry. And I don't think I'm allowed to just be angry. And that's something I didn't notice mattered so much to my being and how I show up.

Me: If you could tell your White or majority culture peers one thing without fear of being misunderstood or silenced, what would it be?

Just listen. Listen and stop being so scared to make mistakes. I think you're so scared of making mistakes that you're trying to be perfect and then that's annoying. Like, you don't know everything, you are going to make mistakes. That's another function of white supremacy. You know, just say the thing that's on your mind. If you think some outlandish stuff, say it. I'm going to say: "That's not okay. Let me tell you why that's not okay." But if you keep it wrapped up in you and you try to be perfect, then you're also not going to become the best version of you. You're not going to dismantle white supremacy. You're going to just keep it going because you're so busy trying to be perfect. So, you know, stop.

Black man: This interviewee works as a business analyst for a large corporation. This conversation picks up with him describing his experience as a racial minority in his company and within his department.

I'm very aware of my surroundings. I'm aware of what I say, how I say it, how it's perceived . . . I stand out in a room. I walk into a room of forty people, and I'm the only Black person, you know. So, they see me, even if I'm not a high man on the totem pole. I can't make a mistake. That's what it feels like. This impending pressure, because if I mess up, I stand out. If somebody else messes up, it's like, "Oh, okay." I've seen that before. So, that's a big thing. Just that pressure of making sure that if I make a mistake it needs to be a good mistake. I can't crash and burn, because they see me.

Me: How do you navigate feeling that pressure?

It's a lot of stress sometimes. I've picked up certain habits, like rubbing my hands a little bit. It's like I don't get to be like everybody else. I know one guy who has seven thousand unread emails. I kid you not. But I'm like, I have fifty, and I need to make sure I reply to each one so that I don't get a bad reputation. So, that's an extra thing.

Another thing is . . . I can't show that I'm frustrated, because I'm a Black man. I don't want to come off as an angry black guy. So, that becomes another thing: How do I do this graciously? How do I point people in the right direction? How do I hold them accountable?

Me: Can you be yourself in this environment?

No, I can't. If I was myself, I'd be rubbing some people the wrong way. If I was being myself, I would communicate more directly. I would work to solve problems on the spot. But I can't be that way here. It would rub people the wrong way.

Korean American woman: This interviewee has a background in corporate America, but switched up her career to work for an international, faith-based nonprofit. She is a manager-level leader within the organization.

Me: Have you ever been in the racial minority in your workplace?

I've always been the minority in all my workspaces.

Me: Tell me what that has been like.

The first six to eight months of a job, because I'm step-ping into majority white contexts, I'm kind of observing the dynamics of the office. What the language is. How people speak to each other. What the joking is like. Because it's pretty different from how I interact with other Korean American friends. I use the adjustment period to sit back and learn the dynamics before engaging. And then it's a process of assimila-tion, because that's what works and that's the expectation of being a minority coming in. Especially as an Asian. It's hard because it's inbred from my parents—as an immigrant, you come in, you work hard, don't get into trouble. But coupled with larger society, there are the expectations put onto Asians that we should play that role.

Me: Have you ever experienced microaggressions in this setting?

I had been experiencing microaggressions for a while, but didn't realize it. Soon after I was hired, my hiring boss told me she was looking specifically for an Asian American to fill the role because we're really hardworking and we get stuff done at a quicker pace than other ethnicities. I thought it was a compliment at first, but when I look back, it's like, "Wow, okay. That's really offensive." It takes a piece out of you every time you hear it. I ended up going through a really angry phase for a long time, and I still dip into it from time to time.

It's really devaluing. The intention is not bad and they're not trying to purposefully hurt you, but the impact of those words or that kind of ignorance starts taking a toll after a while.

I see it more as I go up the ladder. The White male is at the top of the pyramid. Seeing the amount of grace and benefit of doubt that's given to majority culture, first the men and then the women, and then being toward the bottom of that ladder as a person of color and a woman, it's been really difficult. They expect you to be hardworking, but they don't platform you well or set you up to succeed. So, it makes it hard to get promoted. If a White coworker makes the same mistake as me, it's not considered a ding. But for me, it's considered underperformance.

Me: What are the biggest diversity gaps you see?

We talk a good game, there's a lot of verbiage, like: "This is not who we are. We want to do better." But when it comes down to actual decisions that are made, diversity is not included in that conversation. The gap of, "We want to recruit and have more people of color come through our process," but then they are not really willing to budge on how to fund those positions because it's entirely fed and led by majority culture. You're building a structure saying, "We're trying to be inclusive," but none of the structures allow for that to happen. And then we blame the people of color for not having the right tools.

There's only one senior leader in a decision-making role who is a person of color. Everyone else, all the other people of color, are consultants. And then members of majority culture claim those ideas as their own. For majority culture, they want to hold to their positions, and they want it to be seen as a gift to us that we've been invited into those conversations. But they then present our ideas as their own. They say one thing, but it's not what they really want.

Me: Can you be yourself in this environment?

No. Because of fragility and how I've seen majority culture react. Even though I'm learning to be more of myself, everything has to be within the context of what's comfortable for White people.

Me: If there was one thing you could tell your majority culture or White peers without fear of being misunderstood or silenced, what would it be?

We already show you grace. You're asking for people of color to be more gracious and trusting. But you don't even understand the amount of grace we already give you every day.

A MOMENT TO PAUSE

As the interviewer, there were many places where I had to stop and take a deep breath with each interviewee. It's likely you found yourself doing the same while reading the experiences of the interviewees. Their collective voices merit another intentional pause and a deep breath.

Seriously.

Pause.

Take a deep breath.

Take a moment to note which story, phrase, or thought resonates with you the most. It could resonate because it's challenging. It could resonate because it pricked your heart in a certain way. Maybe it was a gut punch. Maybe you recognized something in the leadership of your organization, and you know it is causing similar pain. Capture whatever stands out to you and sit with it for a moment. Reread the voice (or voices) that resonated most with you. Why? What does it mean?

If you are a White person, take a moment to consider the BIPOC who show up to your workplace every day. Maybe they are people on your team, or comanagers or directors who lead alongside you. Research shows they are likely experiencing some aspect of the emotions, trauma, and difficulties as the people from the stories shared here. Please don't go ask them about it. Sharing our stories is tender work, and should happen in the context of trusting relationships. Too often, a White person's eagerness to hear the stories of their coworkers from Black, Asian, Latino/a, and Indigenous communities causes more harm. You can, however, pause and consider how their daily work experience might be drastically different, and more difficult, than your own.

If you are a person of color reading these stories, I have no doubt you're glimpsing your perspective and experiences reflected here. While these experiences are heartbreaking and painful, I hope you feel a little less alone. As I interviewed these people and analyzed their stories for this book, I repeatedly found myself overwhelmed and saddened by the weight of what we carry each day. I also found immense gratitude in hearing my experience echoed in the experiences of others. Be sure to take time to care for yourself. Unearthing painful experiences is exhausting work, especially if you've suppressed these experiences in order to survive, to maintain relationships, to protect your reputation, or to keep your job. Caring for yourself in the midst of this is essential. Some would even say it's revolutionary.

HARMONIZING THE VOICES

Data analysis of these interviews reveals multiple, recurring themes of note.

Theme #1—
Emotional Labor and the Psychological Toll

Many interviewees gave voice to the extra emotional labor required to simply do our jobs at work every day. (I say *our* because this is my experience, too.) There is the emotional labor of smiling through uncomfortable and offensive interactions. The emotional labor of managing our own biases and the biases of others. The emotional labor of suppressing our counternarratives to be seen as a team player. The emotional labor of downplaying our true thoughts and feelings to avoid being stereotyped as "angry" or "difficult." There is also the emotional and psychological toll of having to work out the sadness, anger, frustration, and disrespect we feel on an ongoing basis while trying to maintain perfect composure on the outside. This is, of course, on top of doing the job we are paid to do.[5]

What would it take to create environments where BIPOC can do their best work without the ongoing distraction and burden of racism and white supremacy culture?

Theme #2—
The Pressure to Perform Perfectly

Multiple interviewees spoke of the pressure to perform at a higher standard than their White counterparts. For many people of color, we know our work is scrutinized more harshly than others. There is less grace for mistakes made and balls dropped. There is less room for bad days, down moments, or off-seasons.

In my own experience, I have seen White leaders of organizations go on for months of making poor leadership decisions, experiencing distraction, and losing sight of important goals. However, if I, as a Black woman, have one week—or even a few days—of being "off my game" for any reason, my competency, focus, or commitment to the work is immediately called into question.

What would it be like if we created as much space for the humanity of people of color as we do for White people in our organizations?

Theme #3—
Navigating Assaults on Our Dignity

Efforts to create racially diverse organizations are not about metrics, money, and marketing. These efforts hinge on your ability to affirm and value the dignity of every single person you meet. However, as the stories shared here indicate, many people of color in predominately white institutions endure daily assaults on their personhood in direct and indirect ways. Whether it's through microaggressive comments, power plays, and creating hostile environments, or by demanding for change to happen on the timeline best suited for those in power . . . the assault is pervasive. Destructive. Dehumanizing.

What would it take for majority white organizations, and the people who lead them, to take responsibility for the harm their leadership causes? What would it look like to move beyond a "commitment to diversity" to embodying practices of repair?

• • ● ● • •

What would it look like to move beyond a "commitment to diversity" to embodying practices of repair?

• • ● ● • •

Closing Thoughts

In response to these stories, the next best step is to simply believe what you've heard. Believe the stories. Let them settle within you. Let these stories challenge and expand your worldview.

When you encounter stories from new perspectives in your life and leadership, the most generous response is: *Tell me more.* You center marginalized people, and their voices, by believing their stories and following their leadership in creating inclusive organizational cultures.

When Black people, Asian people, Indigenous people, Latino/a people, multiracial people, biracial people, and more raise their voices, offer new insights, push the envelope, or challenge the status quo, trust them and follow their lead.

MOTIVATION MATTERS

- *Insight:* Your motivation for diversifying your team matters.

- *Action:* If your pursuit of racial diversity is about dignifying people and disrupting racism, keep going. If this is about appearing relevant, stop now.

WHEN PURSUING DIVERSITY CAUSES HARM

It was September 2019, and my friend texted to let me know about a breaking news story. The CEO of a prominent media company had come under fire for racial insensitivity and for creating a toxic workplace culture. I instantly began searching for any and every angle I could find on the story. Based on what I gathered, this company was founded by a

young White man who came from an influential family in
the media industry. The company had grown an international reach, but like many start-ups of its kind, the team
mostly reflected the identity and social perspective of the
founder: white, wealthy, male.

As I read the mainstream articles, I navigated my way to
a few blog posts by various people of color who had once
been employed by this company. Reading their stories was
heart-wrenching, as their experiences felt very similar to
my own. I resonated with their fatigue and frustration. I
knew the feeling of constantly assessing how much or how
hard to advocate for your perspective in a creative meeting.
I knew the anxiety of questioning if the feedback I was
given was rooted in bias or in reality. I knew the stress of
trying to do good racial justice advocacy under the banner
of an organization that had so much of its own work to do
internally. Reading their stories felt like skimming through
my own diaries.

In addition to the ways this story connected with me
personally, it also painted a strikingly accurate depiction
of what many well-meaning, do-good organizations face:
an ongoing gap between the relevant, creative face shown
to the world and the often messy, dysfunctional inside,
especially where race and white supremacy are concerned.
The story of this media company is one of countless stories
where we struggle to align our external presentations with
our internal reality (i.e., the narrative battle).

In many ways, this is a human dilemma. We struggle to
live and lead with perfect alignment, congruency, and integrity. However, if your diversity efforts remain in the realm

of what can be seen on the outside, as opposed to what is felt and experienced within your organization, you reinforce patterns of harm.

What does it mean if we've curated a diversity that *looks good* on Instagram, but doesn't *feel good* to the people on your team?

• • ● • •

What does it mean if we've curated a diversity that *looks good* on Instagram, but doesn't *feel good* to the people on your team?

• • ● • •

Shallow diversity can look great from a distance, but it takes a truly good type of racial, ethnic, and cultural diversity to generate positive outcomes for everyone in the organization.

So, what exactly makes pursuing diversity harmful?

Harmful diversity can be challenging to pin down. It often looks, and sometimes feels, like the right move in the beginning. When we become awake to racism and white supremacy, and to the extensive impact racial division has on our lives, we're compelled to start fixing it right away. We kick off diversity programs, hold trainings and workshops, launch affinity groups, and reimagine our hiring pipelines.

These are all good things. Check box. Check box. Check box.

The hang-up is this: If you move too quickly to check boxes, you miss the opportunity to think strategically and holistically about what diversity means for you, your team, and your organization as a whole. Additionally, if your focus is on checking boxes and appearing relevant, you will likely pursue racial diversity in harmful ways instead of in ways that are dignifying, liberating, and sustainable.

Harmful pursuits of diversity are characterized by at least three things:

- Shortsighted urgency
- Resistance to nuance and complexity
- Lack of resistance to systemic oppression (i.e., racism and white supremacy)

The characteristics of white supremacy culture are right at the doorstep of harmful pursuits of diversity: sense of urgency, either/or thinking, fear of open conflict, and more.

Shortsighted Urgency

Harmful pursuits of diversity are often urgent and short-sighted. They are focused on short-term, momentary wins, such as suddenly diversifying a stage for an event or adding diversity as a last-minute priority in a hiring decision. These short-term "solutions" also emerge in the face of crisis moments, including both national crises and organizational, race-related crises.

These types of shortsighted efforts became prevalent during the summer of 2020, when the murders of Ahmaud

Arbery, Breonna Taylor, and George Floyd garnered international attention. There was a massive push toward solving the problem of racial injustice in a variety of forms. Thought leaders spoke up and spoke out about racism. Those who remained silent faced backlash in public and private spaces. The desire for unconscious bias trainings, dialogues, and anti-racism workshops shot through the roof. Communities were desperate to understand the problem of racism and to solve it.

However, if the extent of your racial justice advocacy and your pursuit of a diverse community rises and falls with the tide of news coverage and public outrage, the problem remains. Systemic racism, and the many cultural and organizational challenges it creates, did not unfold overnight. As such, the work needed to reverse these problems requires a long-term and sustained vision, strategy, creativity, and persistence.

Every operational reality within an organization requires a degree of structure and thoughtfulness. Closing the diversity gap—the gap between good intentions and good impact—requires the same degree of intentionality. We cannot achieve our good diversity goals if we relegate the majority of our race-related initiatives to the urgent moment.

Resistance to Nuance and Complexity

Harmful pursuits of diversity are narrowly focused and don't make room for intersectionality. As mentioned previously, intersectionality offers two important insights.

1. Intersectionality gives voice to the ways some people experience privilege and marginalization at the same time based on their social location.
2. Intersectionality gives expression to the way marginalization is compounded for some individuals based on their social location.

For example, in an organization where White male leadership has been the historical norm, diversity initiatives often cater best to the needs of White people (who share the racial identity of the historical leadership) and men of color (who share the gender identity of historical leadership). This leaves gaping holes in the experiences and opportunities afforded to women of color.

When diversity programs do not account for the experiences of the most marginalized, diversity gaps persist. However, when pursuits of diversity cater to the needs of the most marginalized, everyone has the chance to thrive.

At times, it seems as though the largest barrier to embracing the nuance and complexity of human diversity is largely logistical.

Logistically, as we are in the daily grind of doing good work, it is difficult to make space for the complexity of who we are. It's hard to determine how much identity work is even relevant to our daily operations. It takes more conversations, more disagreements, and longer meetings to get everyone on the same page. It also takes a ton of self-awareness, humility, and maturity. This is exhausting work, especially in the short run. Because of these logistical complications, we pare down our expectations of who gets to be a full person in any given room.

Usually, this means members of the majority culture are given an advantage. When you are from the majority culture, your ways of being are the norm. Therefore, anyone who does not come from your culture has to adjust to match that norm for the sake of efficiency. Organizations are rarely structured, practically, to hold space for minority perspectives to emerge.

What would it take for us to create time and space within our organizations for nuanced, complex, and diverse ways of working to come to life? What would change in our weekly routines, our calendars, our quarterly plans? We'd spend more time connecting, listening, and seeking to understand one another. A new kind of workplace environment would be required for these sorts of changes to take place.

Lack of Resistance to Systemic Oppression

Harmful pursuits of diversity fail to advocate for issues that matter to diverse communities, specifically issues like racism, economic injustice, and immigration reform. It's one thing to say, "I value your presence in my organization." It's another thing altogether to say, "Let's partner together to solve the problems keeping us from thriving together."

Harmful pursuits of diversity say, "Hey, Black people, join our team. We want you here. Your voice and perspective matter to us." Yet, when issues significant to Black communities rise to the surface, like racism in the workplace or police brutality, harmful pursuits of diversity remain silent. They shy away from speaking up, from being "too political," from taking a side when Black lives and well-being are clearly on the line.

Comparisons could be made for other communities. It's one thing to add Latina voices to your team; it's another to concern yourself with the brokenness of systems impacting Latino/a families. It's one thing to add Indigenous perspectives to your speaker lineup; it's another to concern yourself with questions of land ownership, land theft, and Indigenous sovereignty.

In one of my interviews, I spoke with an African American woman who spent five years working for a city-based nonprofit serving people experiencing homelessness. When asked about why she left the organization, she said: "A big challenge I had with [my organization] was the unwillingness to address systems. We would never talk about the systems and give [people] the tools [they needed] to be a part of the solution."

It is harmful when our efforts to increase organizational diversity stop short of caring about the systemic issues shaping communities of color in our society. These diversity efforts give an appearance of concern for all people, but in these scenarios, active demonstrations of care are few and far between.

FINDING THE RIGHT PLACE TO BEGIN

Given the prevalence of falling into one of the buckets above (shortsighted urgency, resistance to nuance and complexity, and a lack of resistance to systemic oppression), it can be difficult to know where to begin. I've been there, and I've needed guides to help me find my way.

I'll never forget my first coaching session with one of my racial justice heroes, Dr. Brenda Salter-McNeil. She'd gathered together a cohort of women who were passionate about racial justice, healing, and reconciliation. In our first few moments together, she told the story of a peer who once said to her, "Brenda, the wrong question will always lead to the wrong answer."

The wrong question will always lead to the wrong answer.

· · ● ● · ·

The wrong question will always lead to the wrong answer.

· · ● ● · ·

The idea is simple enough: If we begin our pursuit of diversity asking the wrong questions, then the answers we discover will not work.

If we focus on questions related to diversifying teams, but fail to ask questions about sharing power, we miss the mark.

If we focus on questions about being socially relevant, but fail to ask questions about the history of our current racial condition, we miss the mark.

If we go about the work of changing our hiring pipelines, but fail to ask questions about needed cultural shifts within our organization, we miss the mark again.

The motivation matters.

The origins matter.

Asking the right questions in the beginning of the process of pursuing diversity is an important first step.

A Failed Intervention

It was 2015. I was a member of a large nonprofit organization filled with hundreds of people from various racial and ethnic backgrounds. White people made up the majority, but there was a strong contingency of people of color, too. The racial climate in the United States was tense, to say the least. The Black Lives Matter movement was gaining steam, and our collective awareness of racial injustice was on the rise. Our nonprofit community had been on a journey of learning more about the history and pervasiveness of systemic racism in the United States. In an effort to support others along the way, a friend and I created a daylong training to educate our community on race-related social issues. This training comprised various teaching inputs, dialogue circles, racial affinity groups, and facilitated exercises.

By 2018, hundreds of people had experienced this workshop. As the workshop experience gained momentum, we took the training on the road, creating learning experiences for communities other than our own. It was quite the adventure. I loved seeing the lightbulb moments people experienced in their own racial justice work and leadership.

As I traveled throughout the region to lead these trainings, I began to observe a pattern. An executive leader would ask me to come host a workshop. I would gather my team and lead the training. Following the experience, I'd receive great feedback about the lessons learned and insights discovered. I counted these moments as wins! A shift in mindsets and attitudes was certainly worth celebrating.

However, as I maintained relationships with these communities over time, I realized that, while mindsets and attitudes were changing, organizational cultures and teams were not. The executive teams and leadership boards were still filled with white, male homogeneity. It was as if people only cared about systemic racism during crisis moments. I thought the intervention of training and education was enough to shift a culture. But the long-term impact of these trainings told a different story.

Yes, people were thinking differently, but they weren't leading differently.

The wrong question always leads to the wrong answer.

My intervention, though well meaning and constructive for some, was ultimately a failure. Organizations and leaders were still choosing comfort and maintenance of the status quo over diversity, equity, inclusion, and justice.

So, I returned to the drawing board. I stopped leading the workshops. Some might say, "What a shame. If the trainings were helping even one person, they were worth it." And maybe that's true. But for me, the goal was, and remains, systemic institutional and organizational change.

To get there, I had to find new questions to pursue. I pivoted my work to research. I wanted to know: *If we all care about solving racism, why aren't we leveraging our influence and leadership to actually solve racism? Why aren't we pursuing diversity when there isn't a crisis in the news? What will it take to overhaul who we are in an effort to become something new?*

A Failing Industry

In addition to my own experience of asking the wrong questions and designing an ultimately ineffective intervention, others have also woken up to the ineffectiveness of traditional diversity and inclusion efforts. Despite billions of dollars spent on trainings, workshops, consulting, and strategic plans, most companies and organizations fail to represent the diversity to which they give so much lip service, money, and energy.

One of the best analyses of this dynamic I've encountered is *Diversity, Inc.: The Failed Promise of a Billion-Dollar Business* by journalist Pamela Newkirk. In this book, Newkirk explains why companies and organizations don't see systemic growth toward diversity, despite a stated and ongoing investment in the work.

Some of the reasons she gives include:

1. The work of diversity consulting asks too much of individuals while simultaneously holding them up to vague, difficult-to-measure standards.

In Newkirk's words:

> The crisis-driven workload, heightened demand, and often vague set of desired job qualifications and expected outcomes are among the myriad problems plaguing the growing field of diversity consultancy. These issues are exacerbated by the fact that there's been limited research or agreement on what bias reduction training is and whether it works.[1]

2. Mandatory training feels helpful in the short run, but not in the long run.

Quoting researchers Dobbin and Kalev, Newkirk shares this insight: "Mandatory training" often "trigger[s] a backlash, particularly among White men. Rather than being converted, they often react with anger and resistance."[2]

3. Overall, traditional diversity and inclusion interventions simply don't seem to be working.

As Newkirk outlines:

> There is no shortage of journals and magazines devoted to the issue. . . . There are diversity blogs, and books and boot camps and best practices. . . . Conspicuously lacking, however, is diversity.
>
> This, despite decades of public pledges and the development of pricy apparatus that have resulted, at best, in incremental progress addressing the pervasive exclusion of racial minorities on corporate boards, in executive suites, in Hollywood studios, and before college classrooms.[3]

When I layer Newkirk's research and observations onto my own research and experience as a racial justice educator, the truth is alarmingly clear: "How do we *diversify?*" is the wrong question to ask in the beginning.

There is something more fundamentally awry than our ability to build teams reflecting racial and ethnic diversity.

● ● ●

A Series of Failed Motivations

In addition to failed interventions and a failing industry, there is also a series of failed motivations undermining efforts to racially, ethnically, and culturally diversify organizations: the business case, the moral case, the spiritual case, and the service case. As you read, make note of the cases you've personally found most compelling. Also make note of the cases you've seen operating in the life of your organization.

Case #1—
The Business Case: More diversity equals more money

In January 2018, McKinsey & Company released a popular report stating: "Companies with the most ethnically diverse executive teams—not only with respect to absolute representation but also of variety or mix of ethnicities—are 33 percent more likely to outperform their peers on profitability."[4] This statistic, and many others like it, point to what is often referred to as "the business case for diversity."

The logic is simple: diversity is good business. If you do diversity well, your company will make more money. In researching the business case for diversity, you will also stumble upon countless articles unpacking the ways diverse teams drive innovation and creativity. We experience better, more creative, more interesting results when we have more perspectives creating good work.

On the surface, the business case for diversity has tremendous merit for profit-driven institutions. The tricky part, however, is in how this motivation impacts people. When an entire diversity strategy is constructed for the sake of competitive advantage, people are commodified.[5]

In the business case for diversity, real humans (with real stories, real gifts, real competencies, and real dreams) are treated like tokens and prized possessions. These people are valued for how they make the organization look, but the organization gives little thought to how the workplace environment is impacting them.

At an event I hosted in March 2020, I had the privilege of learning from Xavier Ramey, CEO of Justice Informed, a Chicago-based social impact firm. During his talk, he said:

> I appreciate the business case for diversity. I challenge it. You see, there was a business case for feeding your slaves twice a day too. They work harder. You get more out of them. More innovations on the plantation. It's chattel diversity. It doesn't mean you actually think they're human. It doesn't mean you know how to respect them. It doesn't mean you understand dignity. It means you have once again subjected a human to be valued on the basis of their productive capacity for you.[6]

The business case for diversity is problematic because it's an assault on human dignity. This motivation hinders our ability to do the actual work of seeing people, honoring their gifts, respecting their differences, and making space for the cultures of our organizations to change.

Case #2—

The Moral Case: More diversity is the right thing to do

Many people come to care about issues of race and diversity by way of learning about injustices in the world. I'll never forget being eighteen years old and taking my first flight ever to Chicago for a spring break service trip. While there, I learned about the broken racial history of Chicago and about the role ordinary people could play to set the wrong things right. This moral case for diversity and racial equity is still compelling to me. And yet, it's not a sufficiently strong impetus for creating diverse cultures and organizations.

Why? Because not everyone believes in our collective responsibility to address social injustice. For many people, there is no sense of duty or obligation to resolve issues of racism and white supremacy. Education and training may help close this gap, but research shows, more often than not, when training is mandatory, it causes a backlash. When people become silently resentful toward pursuing diversity, they hinder progress for everyone.

Additionally, when pursuing diversity is a moral imperative, it usually gets relegated to smaller groups within the organization whose focus is consumed with policing bad behavior. The policing leads to more frustration and less trust. Cross-racial relationships are more strained in these environments, and diversity is rarely integrated with the core functions of an organization or team.

If you have strong convictions about diversity and racial justice, you may be thinking, *It shouldn't be this way.* I agree with you. In my dreamworld, every person would understand the devastating and exclusionary impacts of racism and white supremacy, and they would each carry the conviction to do something about these problems. But my experience and the research both tell me this isn't our reality. It's tough to rally people around a movement they don't believe in.

Case #3—
The Spiritual Case: More diversity is what we're designed to pursue

Earlier, I told a story about the training program I created to help organizations understand and respond to the challenges of racism in their community and society. What I didn't mention before is that this was a faith-based organization. As a community, we carried a strong conviction that humans are designed for diverse community and to participate in the healing of the world. This spiritual motivation was rooted in our historical faith tradition.

This is what I call a "spiritual case" for diversity. Many people who participate in spiritual communities also find a spiritual and/or mystical impetus to engage in the work of diversity and resisting racism. While this vision moves people emotionally, and maybe even spiritually, it rarely compels leaders to change the demographic makeup of their teams. It seldom challenges leaders to follow the expertise and wisdom of the most marginalized. In the spiritual case for diversity, it's easy to get lost in feelings and conversation. There is little accountability within this case to actually change organizational realities.

The spiritual case makes for a great TED talk, but this case rarely alters the trajectory of many leaders' paths. It rarely leads to more diverse boards or leadership councils. If anything, leaders in these contexts tend to double down on their power and resist the hard work of transformation. While the spiritual case is a beautiful one, it's not enough to close the gap between good intentions and true cultural change.

Case #4—
The Service Case: More diversity will better serve our community

For many years, my racial justice education work was located in or near Metro Atlanta, Georgia. When attempting to inspire leaders of organizations in my community to racially diversify their teams, I used to say something like this: "If you are committed to serving the city of Atlanta, a place where more than 50 percent of the residents are African American, your team's racial demographics ought to reflect the city."

Companies also use a similar logic related to their customer base: "If we are going to sell to people from X community, then our sales team needs to look like X community."

This is the service case for diversity. It sounds really wonderful, and the service case in particular can lead to the creation of a more diverse team. But this purpose isn't without its limitations.

According to organizational behavior researchers Robin J. Ely and David A. Thomas, when diversity is pursued with this service orientation in mind, it becomes a side project. People of color are used to make the organization look woke and relevant in the eyes of the public or consumer base. It also severely limits how much the "diversity hires" can speak to the core functions of the organization or company.[7]

These limitations perpetuate racial inequality in the workplace as white, majority culture members are allowed to speak to any and every area of the group's functioning, while people of color are only allowed to speak to "diversity-related" functions. While the service case sounds compelling, it doesn't give way to creating a culture of diversity, dignity, and liberation.

The Dignity Case for Pursuing Diversity

Pursuing racial, ethnic, and cultural diversity is about dignifying people. It is about who you value. It's about whose stories and whose lives truly matter to you. This pursuit is not about checking boxes, appearing relevant, or making more money. This work is about creating equitable workplace cultures. This work is also about learning how to resist and disrupt racism and white supremacy.

· · ● ● ● · ·

The dignity case for pursuing diversity says that all people are inherently worthy of respect, safety, encouragement, and support when they arrive at work.

· · ● ● ● · ·

If an organizational culture is creating a harmful impact on the lives of people in the organization, then the organization needs to change.

When you hold human dignity at the forefront of your aspirations to cultivate a racially and ethnically diverse organization, you create an environment where diverse groups of people are encouraged to appreciate and learn from one another. Prioritizing human dignity will challenge you to slow down and to enter into the messiness of relational dynamics. It will force you to evaluate how your origin story and the origin stories of others are shaping your organizational culture.

You stop asking, "How do I diversify my organization?" and you start asking: "How is my organization resisting racism? How are we regularly affirming the dignity of people of color? What are we sacrificing today in order to create a more inclusive organization tomorrow?"

New questions emerge when you put people first. Your strategies and, ultimately, your culture will evolve as a result of asking more dignifying and human-centered questions.

CHOOSE YOUR FRAMEWORK

- *Insight:* There are many frameworks for pursuing organizational culture and diversity, and each has different objectives.

- *Action:* Choose your framework and know why.

DIVERSITY? RECONCILIATION? LIBERATION?

When you set out to racially, ethnically, and culturally diversify your organization, you will find there are many perspectives on what kind of work is worth doing. Various thought leaders and consultants approach the question of diversity in different ways. There's an entire vocabulary dedicated to clarifying what is meant by the pursuit of *diversity*, as opposed to the pursuits of reconciliation, anti-racism, equity, inclusion, belonging, and liberation.

Below is a framework designed to help you think more deeply, creatively, and holistically about what it means for you to pursue racial and ethnic diversity in your organization.

As established in previous chapters, it's important to remember:

- Racism and white supremacy are the root problems. You must continually address and resist these systemic cultural realities.
- The impact of your actions on people of color is more important than your good intentions. You must continually listen to, believe, and follow the leadership of people of color.
- Your motivation for pursuing racial diversity matters. If this work is about you, stop. If this work is about dignifying others, keep going.

With these insights in mind, I present to you *The Diversity to Liberation Framework*. This breakdown has not only helped me think about organizational culture and diversity in new ways, but it has served as a touchpoint to help me understand where others are on the journey. When you know your unique focus, as well as the focuses of those on your team, you are better prepared to find alignment and make progress together.

As a leader, one of the best gifts you can give to others is clarity about where you are taking your organization and why. In unpacking the diagram on the following page, take note of where your focus has been historically. Also, con-sider where your team is currently located on this diagram.

THE DIVERSITY TO LIBERATION FRAMEWORK

In Figure 1, there are three frameworks for pursuing orga-nizational diversity. Each framework asks different sets of questions, engages different vehicles for change, and defines success in varied ways.

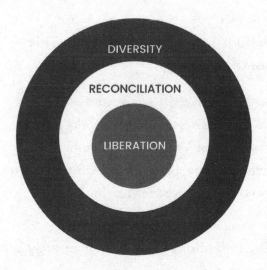

Figure 1

Diversity, in the outermost ring, is defined as "the state of having multiple races, ethnicities, nationalities, and cultural perspectives present on your team"; it is the undeniable pres-ence of difference.

Reconciliation, in the middle ring, is defined as "the ongoing process of restoring authentic and mutually dignifying relationships between people from different racial, ethnic, and cultural perspectives."

Liberation, in the center, is defined as "freedom from oppressive systems, stories, habits, policies, and practices." Liberation is inclusive of anti-racism and various anti-oppressive practices.

FRAME #1: DIVERSITY

Key Questions Leaders Ask When in This Framework:

> How do we diversify our team?
> How do we diversify our networks to help with recruiting non-White team members?
> What makes people from nonwhite backgrounds feel integral to what we are creating?

Where Organizations Focus Their Energy When in This Framework:

> Hiring and retention of non-White candidates
> Tracking various metrics related to diversity
> Ensuring diverse representation in marketing materials
> Strategic positioning for public relations

Vehicles for Changing the Organization:

Hosting implicit bias or unconscious bias trainings

Hiring diversity consultants

Launching employee resource groups

Creating diversity task forces

Success Looks and Feels Like:

Representation—in other words, when you look at the demographic makeup of your organization, you see a variety of races, ethnicities, and cultures represented.

FRAME #2: RECONCILIATION

Key Questions Leaders Ask When in This Framework:

How do we build meaningful cross-racial connections and relationships?

How do we talk about race and diversity in a sustainable way?

Where is racial conflict present on our team and how do we address it?

● ● ●

Where Organizations Focus Their Energy When in This Framework:

Cultivating cross-racial relationships with team members, board members, and vendors

Strengthening internal communications

Learning and understanding histories of different racial and ethnic groups

Building community across lines of racial and ethnic difference

Vehicles for Changing the Organization:

Dialogue

Facilitation

Conflict mediation

Storytelling

Building cultural competency

Success Looks and Feels Like:

Authentic connection—in other words, people from various racial and ethnic backgrounds feel like they are seen and known for who they are, and people practice seeing and knowing those who are unlike themselves.

FRAME #3:
LIBERATION

Key Questions Leaders Ask When in This Framework:

Where is racism at work in our organization?
What role have oppressive systems played in creating the problems our organization is trying to solve?
Are our actions racist or proactively anti-racist?

Where Organizations Focus Their Energy When in This Framework:

Activism
Power
Centering the marginalized
Reparations

Vehicles for Changing the Organization:

Activism
Reflection
Therapy
Accountability
Imagination

Success Looks and Feels Like:

Organizational and systemic change—in other words, organizations operate in anti-racist, anti-oppressive, and liberating ways; all people are invited to participate in dismantling oppressive systems and reimagining society.

Personal growth—in other words, team members from various racial backgrounds are growing in their racial and ethnic identities, as well as in their understanding of how to dismantle oppressive systems.

	Diversity	Reconciliation	Liberation
Questions	How do we diversify our team? How do we diversify our networks to help with recruiting non-White team members? What makes people from nonwhite backgrounds feel integral to what we are creating?	How do we build meaningful cross-racial connections and relationships? How do we talk about race and diversity in a sustainable way? Where is racial conflict present on our team and how do we address it?	Where is racism at work in our organization? What role have oppressive systems played in creating the problems our organization is trying to solve? Are our actions racist or proactively anti-racist?

Focus	Hiring and retention of non-White candidates Tracking various metrics related to diversity Ensuring diverse representation in marketing materials Strategic positioning for public relations	Cultivating cross-racial and cross-cultural relationships Strengthening internal communications Learning and understanding histories of different racial and ethnic groups Building community across lines of racial and ethnic difference	Practicing social and cultural activism Redistributing and rebalancing power Centering the marginalized Paying and practicing reparations
Vehicles	Hosting implicit bias or unconscious bias trainings Hiring diversity consultants Launching employee resource groups Creating diversity task forces	Dialogue Facilitation Conflict mediation Storytelling Building cultural competency	Education Reflection Therapy Accountability Imagination
Success	Representation	Authentic connection	Personal growth and organizational change

At various points in my journey, different frameworks from this diagram were at the forefront of my leadership. When I was fresh out of college, I was incredibly passionate about reconciliation. I wanted to build an intentional community where individuals were growing in their racial identities and cultural perspectives, and learning how to talk about race in generative ways.

After a few years in the reconciliation framework, I became curious about diversity. I wanted to see organizations reflect and represent the rich diversity of our communities on their stages, on their advisory boards, and on their leadership teams.

As the problems of racism and white supremacy became more glaring, especially in the organizational context, liberation became nonnegotiable. Everything else felt like a Band-Aid.

In addition to thinking about diversity work more critically, I began evaluating my own health and wellness as a Black woman in the world. If my health and wellness decline in an effort to "diversify teams" or "diversify organizations," then what has truly been gained? Yes, maybe the organization looks more inclusive and maybe the teams do change, but at what cost? I started to wonder, *If Black lives matter, does that include mine?*

Consider how these various frameworks impact your efforts to racially, ethnically, and culturally diversify your team. Is pursuing diversity enough? Are you in a season where reconciliation needs to be prioritized? How can you integrate liberating activity into this process?

Here is a case study on how the three frameworks operated together in the context of a real organization: Plywood People.

Case Study: Plywood People

Plywood People is a nonprofit in Atlanta, Georgia, leading a community of start-ups doing good. The organization began a little more than a decade ago when the founder, Jeff Shinabarger, set out to create a community of social entrepreneurs looking for connection, training, and support to launch their ideas. What began as a gathering of a hundred people at an event called Plywood Presents grew into an entire ecosystem of creativity, courage, and compassion. Through this community, everyday people find the gumption and training they need to launch or scale their businesses, organizations, or projects.

I joined Plywood People in 2017 as the event leader. At the time, the organization was majority white. To change this reality, the leadership made an intentional decision to move toward diversifying every aspect of the organization, beginning with the board and team.

When I joined, many of our conversations about race were in the *diversity* framework. Racially diversifying the team and board happened first. In an effort to bolster diverse representation within the community of entrepreneurs as a whole, we experimented with launching an affinity group for leaders of color. When planning events, we sought out diverse representation in terms of gender, age, sexual orientation, race, and industry. Diversity became a common and consistent priority: How do we make sure every piece of our work represents the community we are striving to lead and serve?

In the midst of intentionally and methodically diversifying every part of our community, we began pursuing reconciliation as well. This involved countless conversations, vulnerability, addressing conflict, and holding space for differing perspectives. These conversations were rarely planned. They happened over the course of a meal or during team meetings. Normalizing conversations about race and identity played a huge role in strengthening our team's ability to talk about race in ongoing and constructive ways.

We tested out many experiments and strategies between 2017–2019. I held a focus group with women of color to better understand their challenges and experiences of the Plywood community. We attended anti-racism workshops to gain fresh perspectives on how racism was functioning in our organization. During our largest events of the year, we invited speakers and thought leaders to share about diversity, anti-racism work, and more. The board of directors read books together and pursued further education in their own spheres of influence. It was a season of tremendous internal growth and learning.

In 2020, a couple of additional shifts happened. A new director of operations was hired to colead the organization with the executive director. This role was filled by a Black woman. This not only increased diverse representation, but it shifted power within the organization—a move toward liberation.

Also, in 2020, the team began discussing what it would look like to adopt an organizational value for pursuing diversity and anti-racism. Adding a new value created a standard to which the organization could be held accountable.

For Plywood People, the movement from diversity to reconciliation to liberation was not linear. There were many overlapping actions, innumerable conversations, and hundreds of little decisions required to pave the way for ongoing, lasting change.

Decisions such as:

- What books are we requiring for this summer's internship?
- We need to increase Asian American thought leadership in our next event series. Let's create a budget line item for this.
- The only Black person on our team is feeling isolated. Let's pay to send her to a conference for Black leaders.
- We have a board meeting next month. Let's bring in a person to train us on diversity and culture-building. We'll definitely pay them.
- I'm looking to train my team on hospitality in the service industry. Where can I find hospitality books written by women or people of color?

Overlapping actions. Innumerable conversations. Hundreds of little decisions.

These changes don't happen overnight. There is always more work to do. When you understand where you are and cast a vision for where you are headed, you create an opportunity for every team member to lend their efforts toward making a difference.

LOOKING AT THE FRAMEWORK
IN ANOTHER WAY

One way to begin identifying diversity gaps in your organization is to discover where these frameworks overlap in your context. Check out the Venn diagram in Figure 2.

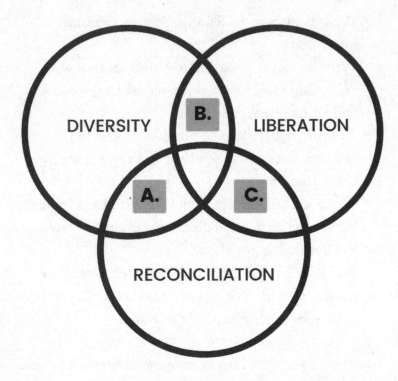

Figure 2

In this model, there are clear points of overlap between the different frameworks.

Where **diversity and reconciliation** overlap at (A.), you experience the richness of diversity and connection across lines of cultural difference. You also get to build the interpersonal skills required to navigate race-related tensions. These spaces have likely pursued consulting support, hosted affinity groups or dialogues spaces, and have practiced addressing race-related conflict, either within the team or in the world.

What is missing from the *diversity-reconciliation* space is a power-analysis (thinking critically about how power is hoarded or shared), an understanding of systemic oppression (learning how to see and name oppressive activities in your midst), and activism (putting your resources and bodies on the line to resist racism and white supremacy).

Where **diversity and liberation** overlap at (B.), you gain access to new perspectives, you are actively involved in significant social causes, you work with therapists and healers to address internalized oppression, and you learn how to imagine a new kind of world. One of the environments in which the *diversity-liberation* frame is most evident is on social media. If you're intentional, you can curate an entire feed reflecting the stories and experiences of people who are unlike you (i.e., diversity). On social media, you can also find countless ways to get involved in activism work, whether by calling elected officials, signing petitions, amplifying voices through posts and hashtags, or donating money (i.e., practicing liberation).

What's occasionally missing from the *diversity-liberation* frame is an authentic, cross-racial connection. It's one thing to post #blacklivesmatter. It's another thing to sit down with the Black people in your life, listen to their stories, wrestle with your own narratives, and practice talking about race.

I frequently find myself in scenarios where it feels like I'm really "doing the work," because I am well versed in multiple perspectives and because I'm doing my part to dismantle internalized white supremacy. And yet, when a peer of a different racial background wants to have a direct, in-person conversation about race, politics, or anything potentially contentious, I freeze. Or get angry. Or shut down. Learning to engage the complexity of real relationships is essential; it's a muscle you have to build.

Where **reconciliation and liberation** overlap at (C.), you get access to much cultural goodness. You engage with history, you have meaningful conversations, and you pursue social transformation. Where reconciliation and liberation overlap, you not only learn about different cultural perspectives, you're able to understand how systems of oppression have shaped the histories and narratives of various communities.

What is typically missing from the *reconciliation-liberation* space is an ability to measure and track progress. The ability to set defined goals with clear metrics is integral to making progress on an organizational level. In the most culture-shaping movements for justice and liberation, lasting impact has come from measured and precise policy change. You need the spreadsheets. You need the diversity dashboards. You need a plan for changing institutional policy. All these activities make our reconciliation-liberation work even more dynamic and sustainable.

In an ideal scenario, you would be in the middle of the Venn diagram—in the place where diversity, reconciliation, and liberation work together to create the cultures of the future. This is a culture in which representation, authentic connection, personal growth, and systemic change are integrated into the core functions of how you lead and how your organization operates. Here is a case study of an organization that regularly integrates these three frameworks.

• • ● ● ● • •

Diversity, reconciliation, and liberation work together to create the cultures of the future.

• • ● ● ● • •

Case Study: Creative Reaction Lab

Creative Reaction Lab, founded by Antionette Carroll, is a nonprofit organization based in St. Louis, Missouri, that exists to "educate, train and challenge Black and Latino/a youth (and allies) to become leaders in designing healthy and racially equitable communities."[1] My first, in-person introduction to the Creative Reaction Lab was an immersive workshop their team curated and I attended.

Antionette and her team were on the forefront of creating a groundbreaking design thinking practice called Equity-Centered Community Design (ECCD). In this design thinking process, you learn how to understand your user, design a solution, rapidly prototype, and get user feedback. What sets the ECCD paradigm apart from other design thinking methodologies is that you also learn how to acknowledge, address, and respond to the societal inequities present in any given design problem. It's a remarkable paradigm shift, and I wanted to learn more.

In June 2019, Creative Reaction Lab took its ECCD content on the road, hosting immersive weekend experiences to teach practitioners of all kinds the ins and outs of solving design challenges in this equity-centered way. I traveled to New York City to participate and was thrilled to be in a room with so many creative, thoughtful, justice-minded people.

Over the course of the weekend, I learned new information from the various training and teaching inputs. But my biggest takeaways were simply from experiencing how Antionette and her co-facilitator, Hilary Sedovic, facilitated the space. Here were my observations:

- At the beginning of the workshop, extensive time and space were allotted to share, critique, and establish group agreements. We discussed our boundaries and expectations for communication, addressing problems, and using language to dignify everyone's experiences. With nearly fifty people in the room, this took time. But every voice had the chance to be heard.

- During the workshop, in real time, Hilary and Antionette would change their presentation slides to capture and respond to insights from people in the room. They had an agenda and told us what to expect throughout the day, but everything was amendable as needs and ideas arose in real time. They demonstrated immense flexibility and decentralized their power as facilitators.

- If and when something harmful, exclusionary, or offensive happened during our time together, Antionette and Hilary would quickly and publicly acknowledge the harm caused and accept responsibility for any negative impact they had. They would then move to repair the harm by making amends, changing the environment, or adjusting the presentation. They prioritized their impact over their good intentions.

- Over the course of the weekend, they normalized discussing the complexities and nuances of identity. It was normal to remind people of the correct pronouns to use. It was normal to discuss our experiences of racism, ageism, and ableism. We regularly discussed what made us feel seen and included or rejected and excluded. Perfectionism wasn't the priority. Being seen, dignified, and given space to contribute authentically are what mattered most.

- Last, the environment was an iterative, ever-evolving space. We honored the lived experiences of our bodies and the bodies of others. We talked plainly about systems of oppression, and both the privileges they afforded some and the barriers they created for others. We were able to grow and change together. Not because we were all the same—we definitely were *not*. But we experienced a degree of flexibility, intentionality, and freedom I haven't experienced in an organizational context since.

This immersive workshop embodied what a culture of the future looks and feels like.

It was diverse: People identified in multiple ways, racially and ethnically, as well as in terms of gender, age, and ability.

It was reconciliatory: Authentic relationships were cultivated across lines of difference.

It was liberating: Power was shared, harm was addressed and repaired, and issues of social injustice were grappled with and responded to.

LONG-TERM ENGAGEMENT

A couple of years ago, I had the privilege of learning from Dr. Darnisa Amante-Jackson. Dr. Amante-Jackson is the co-founder and CEO of the Disruptive Equity Education Project, also known as DEEP. As an educational and racial equity strategist (and a leadership lecturer at Harvard), Dr. Amante-Jackson is known for guiding leaders and organizations toward greater equity and transformation.

Dr. Amante-Jackson taught me—from the time they desire to pursue greater diversity to the time they have an organization where practicing reconciliation and liberation is the integrated norm—it takes a community eight to ten years to experience real change. *Eight to ten years.*

You are playing a long game here. To make progress, you have to develop new leadership skills and priorities to take you where your organization needs to go. Shallow diversity is no longer enough. Flourishing and freedom for all people is the new standard. While there are strategies to employ and experiments to try, there are no shortcuts or silver bullets. The burden is on you to understand how oppression has shaped your organizational culture. It's on you to learn how your team is navigating an ever-evolving social landscape.

It's on you to refuse to do business as usual. It's on you to unlearn the old and embrace the new.

The good news is that you are not on this journey alone. The next few chapters explore new values to adopt, personal life habits to change, and organizational practices to help you along the way.

Need help determining which framework is primary in your organization? At the end of this book, in Appendix A, you will find the Diversity to Liberation Assessment. You can implement this tool not only to discover your organizational framework, but to learn the frameworks of your team members as well.

You can also access the assessment online at www.the diversitygap.com/assessment.

EMBRACE
CULTURAL CHANGE

- *Insight:* You have to adopt new, more liberating values and behaviors if you want diverse groups of people to flourish as they follow you.

- *Action:* Practice liberation; embody cultural change.

THE POWER OF CULTURE

My coworker and I signed up to attend a workshop on naming racism and transforming organizations.[1] As friends and team members, we were committed to increasing our capacity to confront and dismantle oppressive systems in our organization and in the world.

To kick off this learning experience, the facilitators asked the group to name the characteristics of the dominant culture in the United States. As is usually the case in these group learning experiences, the ball started rolling slowly but surely. Eventually, people began calling out characteristics from across the room:

Male
White
Heterosexual
Christian
Middle-aged
Married
Cisgendered
Wealthy
Formally educated

As people called out characteristics, the facilitators captured them on a large poster at the front of the room. I took a deep breath as I read the list. The founder of the organization I worked for, and the founders of many other values-driven organizations in my orbit, were led by people who checked each and every one of those boxes. I was also struck by the realization that the people most often considered "successful" in my community also checked every box on the list.

It made me wonder, *Have the leaders in my network actually been the creative, inspiring, and talented people I was told they are, or do they simply embody what our culture values most?*

If the dominant culture in the United States values and celebrates a person who embodies this list of characteristics, then of course it will be easier for them to start companies, organize nonprofits, write books, record albums, and be elected to political office. It's not about *talent*; it's about how white supremacy rewards being a certain kind of human.

Identifying this pattern isn't about shaming people or making anyone feel negative about who they are. Identifying this pattern highlights the power of culture to affirm, validate, and propel some people forward while actively creating isolation, barriers, and rejection for others.

This dominant cultural vision not only creates challenges, some of which are truly life-threatening for people who don't check these boxes, it also creates an impossible standard to live up to for those who *do* fit the boxes. There are so many stories of White men being crushed under the weight of the expectation to lead, save, and change the world. This cultural pressure doesn't serve anyone. We are all in need of liberation.

LIBERATION FROM WHAT?

In chapter one, we did a deep dive into racism and white supremacy culture. Racism and white supremacy are historical systems that create an advantage for people from white racial backgrounds at the expense of people of color. This is one system we need liberation from (see Figure 3). Here are additional oppressive systems at work in many values-driven, do-good organizations.

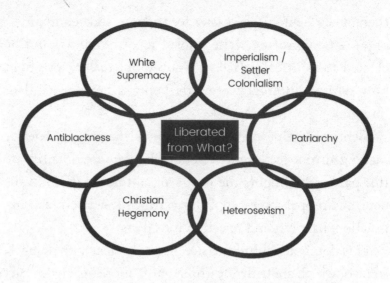

Figure 3

Patriarchy

Patriarchy is a historical system in which men hold most of
the social, political, and economic power. It is also a system
from which women are largely excluded. To see this at work,
research who holds the most political offices, who leads most
businesses, nonprofits, and churches, and who owns the most
money and material resources in the United States.

Heterosexism

This refers to systems that deny, disparage, or reject nonhet-
erosexual relationships, activities, identities, or behaviors. It
also actively advantages heterosexual orientations, relationships, activities, and behaviors.

Antiblackness

This form of racism continually denies Black humanity. It's the other side of the "white supremacy" coin. In this system, not only is it considered best to be White, it's also considered the worst to be Black. Given the prevalence of colorism and light-skinned privilege across the globe, antiblackness exists not only in US society, but in societies all over the world.

Christian Hegemony

Christian hegemony has nothing to do with one's personal beliefs or expression of spirituality. Christian hegemony refers to the ways in which Christianity, as a dominant religion in the United States, sets the standard for who "belongs" here and who does not.

Imperialism and Settler Colonialism

Imperialism refers to the expansion of territory via military power or diplomacy. Inherent within imperialist thinking is a sense of entitlement to take over land, people, and resources. Imperialism goes hand in hand with settler colonialism because settler colonialism is also a system in which the powerful strive to replace Indigenous peoples with a settler society. This imperial, colonizing impulse can be seen in the gentrification of cities and neighborhoods, often shrouded in phrases like "taking new land," "pioneering new frontiers," and "embracing manifest destiny."

Intersectionality is especially relevant in light of these overlapping systems. Based on your social location (e.g., your race, ethnicity, gender, ability status, military status, etc.), you will experience the privileges or barriers of each of these systems differently.

Culture at large, and your organizational culture in particular, are always at work to either maintain these systems or to disrupt them.

CULTURE OVER EVERYTHING

Culture comprises stories, values, behaviors, artifacts, assumptions, and priorities. Culture is a powerful vehicle for transformation. When you articulate values, you're making clear choices about the behaviors and priorities of your organization. As Patrick Lencioni, a renowned business leader, describes it, your values are another way of expressing "how you behave."[2]

Culture is fascinating not only in the tangible ways it's expressed, the stories people tell, the values leaders name, and the heroes communities celebrate, but also in the intangible details. Culture is essence—a feeling, a knowing, and an experience. When you think of Disney World, a sense of magic comes to mind. When you think of Nike, thoughts of excellence and high performance emerge. Even cities have a culture: New York is different from Seattle, which is different from Chicago, which is different from

Los Angeles. In this way, culture conveys identity. It is also a communicator of who belongs in any given community, and who does not.

While culture, and its various attributes, can function as a vehicle for organizational change, it's also the most compelling reason for maintaining the status quo. I've heard countless leaders say, "We want to pursue greater diversity, but we don't want to compromise who we are." What they are really saying is: "We value our culture as it is. How can we pursue diversity without changing too much?"

The good news is, if you already have a defined and compelling culture (i.e., clearly stated values, behaviors you reinforce through celebration, key stories you repeatedly tell, and catchphrases to remind people who you are and what you're about), then you're off to a great start. Having a clearly defined culture will help you imagine a different way to function as you dive into the values of a new and liberating culture.

The challenging news is, if your organization and the culture you celebrate have routinely privileged one kind of person over others, then embracing new, more liberating values will require fundamental changes. Typically, the values you've stated are not the ones hindering your ability to create a diverse and liberating culture. It is the unstated, assumed values you bring to the table and establish as normal. The unstated, assumed, and often unconscious values you carry are the ones you have to reckon with the most.

One way to begin identifying who your culture currently serves is to ask a few simple questions.

- Does my organization have an archetypal team member, client, or community member? If so, what is that person like?
- Who do we celebrate as heroes in our organizational culture? Who do we villainize or criticize?
- Who is represented in the stories we repeatedly tell? Who is left out?
- Who writes our organization's values and key messages? Whose voice is amplified? Whose voice is ignored, silenced, or simply not represented?

Answering these questions will help you identify whom your culture affirms the most and whom your culture affirms the least.

VALUES OF LIBERATING CULTURE

Values are a helpful way to talk about culture because they give us containers for engagement, reflection, and practice. To find and unpack values of a liberating culture, I looked beyond the traditional, nine-to-five boundaries of organizational life. Some of these values are found in our families or faith communities. Some of them exist around bonfires and dining room tables with friends. When values lead to liberation in one area of life, there is potential for those values to lead to liberation in our organizational lives as well.

Each value listed below includes a description, a story or two, and a few practices you can exercise to make the value more your own. It may feel counterintuitive to consider these values in your work and leadership context, or to jump from reading about a new value to immediately considering how to put the value into practice. Don't get lost in merely thinking about these values; values are only as useful as your ability to practice them. As you read, take note of one or two values you would like to try on first.

#1. Embodiment

Take a deep breath. Feel the air fill your lungs. Place your hand on your belly and feel it rise and fall as you take another breath. Your life and your leadership live in your body. In this physical, creaturely, smelly, high-maintenance, please-feed-me thing.

When I first began working with an executive coach, one of my earliest discoveries was how impatient and hostile I had been toward my body. I viewed my body as a commodity, only valuing her for what she could produce for me. I would push through days without eating enough. I would rarely pause to make sure I was giving her enough oxygen through my breathing. I did not love or honor my body for the home, vessel, and trusted companion she's been to me all these years.

Embodiment is the ongoing practice of seeing, honoring, and celebrating the presence of our physical bodies. We cannot dignify the bodies and lived experiences of others if we haven't cultivated a felt appreciation for our own bodies and lived experiences.

Do It: Embodiment

- Build your schedule around the felt needs of your body (food, water, rest, etc.).
- Take a moment at the beginning of meetings for people to take deep breaths and experience their aliveness.
- Pause in the middle of meetings for those who are able to stand and stretch.
- Take "bio breaks" during meetings to honor people's needs to use the restroom and/or grab water or a snack.
- Celebrate when people take days off to care for their bodies due to sickness, physical distress, or general exhaustion.

Embodiment is a liberating value because it affirms the goodness and dignity of all bodies. It also honors the body's limits by resisting the oppressive cultures of extraction, commodification, and exploitation.

#2. Sharing Power

Traditional leadership structures are hierarchical. There is a clear authority figure and a designated chain of command. This leadership structure is highly normalized, and questioning this structure can be uncomfortable. But what if there are more collaborative ways to share power and lead?

I once interviewed a dear friend named Kelly. At the time, she worked for an education nonprofit whose mission was to strengthen the emotional well-being of teachers. As Kelly talked about the structure of this organization, I learned it was not a hierarchy, but a *holacracy*. A holacracy is a decentralized management and decision-making structure. Members are not "employees" but "partners." Each partner knows his or her goals, and if those goals are not met, it is discussed among the group. As such, this team of twelve to fifteen people had cultivated a high degree of trust. Additionally, Kelly (who is an Indigenous woman) shared how the culture of this team created space for her to find her voice and own her ideas. Sharing power equalizes opportunities for influence. It also makes room for new voices and perspectives to shape an organization's culture.

• • ● ● ● • •

Sharing power equalizes opportunities for influence.

• • ● ● ● • •

Do It: Sharing Power

- Pay everyone on your team the same salary; no position is more important or more valuable than another.

- Cultivate group accountability, where each team member knows everyone else's goals and responsibilities.
- Prioritize specific deliverables (like projects completed and goals reached) over less tangible indicators of work (like how many hours are spent at the office).
- Give people freedom and resources to try out new ideas or projects in their own way, as opposed to following *your* way.
- Create a nonhierarchical leadership team of three to five people, among whom decision making is truly a shared endeavor.

Sharing power is a liberating value because it is the opposite of the white supremacist cultural value of power hoarding. Sharing power indicates one's confidence in the abundance of resources available in any given scenario.

#3. Practice over Perfection

This value is all about embracing the risk and practice of change. Leaders often struggle with the fear of "getting it wrong." They fear saying the wrong thing, doing the wrong thing, selecting the wrong training, hiring the wrong person. The list goes on and on. This fear of failure, and the desire to do diversity work perfectly and without sacrifice, is paralyzing. When you embrace practice over perfection, the fear of getting it wrong does not keep you from pursuing what's right. When you choose practice over perfection, you are admitting:

"I don't know everything; I'm guaranteed to get a lot of things wrong, but I'm here. I will take the risk to do better."

It's a posture of humility, of surrender, of openness to feedback, and of experimentation. This value acknowledges that none of us ever "arrive" at some finally liberated place. Rather, we choose to stay on the path.

Do It: Practice over Perfection

- Ask your team, either in person or via anonymous survey, what diversity gaps they see and how they think your organization might address them.
- Find a way to get involved in a community unlike your own, where you are positioned as the learner, not the expert or leader.
- Talk to a friend or loved one about a time when you said or did the wrong thing. Discuss how you would do it differently if given the chance.
- Select one of the systems of oppression outlined above and commit one year to learning more about how it operates.
- When called out for saying or doing the wrong thing, acknowledge the feedback, accept responsibility for your impact, and learn from those harmed what it would take to repair the damage.

Practice over perfection is a liberating value, because it's a counternarrative to the perfectionism plaguing many organizational cultures. It's fundamentally invitational and holds space for the complexity of the human experience.

#4. Accountability

Accountability is about consequences and rewards. Consequences and rewards determine the choices people make each and every day. Do I buckle my seat belt, or no? Do I go to work today, or not? Do I eat this or eat that? Do I say this or say that? We are constantly weighing costs and benefits.

When I work with organizations, I find that many people already have the information they need to make changes. What they lack is incentive. In these scenarios, staying the same is valued more highly than the rewards of change. This is especially true for those who benefit from exploitative, oppressive, or extractive systems.

Accountability forces a reckoning. This is where the rubber meets the road.

Do It: Accountability

- When setting diversity goals, predetermine "celebrations" for the goals you reach and "course corrections" for the goals you don't reach. Regularly update your team and community on your progress.
- Build a diversity task force whose responsibility it is to keep your diversity goals integrated and on track (more on this in future chapters).

- Commit to one or two peer relationships where you intentionally learn about systems of oppression, and practice liberation, together.
- When you receive difficult feedback, write it down and choose a future time to follow up.
- Practice radical honesty and transparency, resisting the temptation to make facts appear better than they are.

Accountability is a liberating value because it creates checks and balances; it creates a pathway to address harm within the organization and challenge leadership to give more than lip service to their desire to change.

#5. Emotional Authenticity

Given the overemphasis on productivity present in many workplace cultures, especially those in the start-up world, there is a tendency to downplay or ignore the presence of emotions. They are viewed as irrelevant or inefficient. It is tempting to power through the day, paying little attention to the feelings you are experiencing.

During moments of racial crisis, suppressing authentic emotion is debilitating. Hiding or suppressing authentic emotion also creates a culture of dishonesty. You cannot build trust on a foundation of countless little lies.

Emotional authenticity makes honest interactions possible. Being aware of, and honest about, how we feel helps us build trust and set appropriate boundaries. These skills are essential when addressing contentious topics or oppressive dynamics in the workplace.[3]

Do It: Emotional Authenticity

- Before, during, and after conversations about race or other contentious topics, use a feelings wheel to help people articulate their experience.
- Practice journaling to increase emotional self-awareness.
- Practice mindfulness and meditation (apps are great for this).
- Identify one or two peers with whom you can be transparent and self-reflective.
- When strong, difficult emotions arise, go for a walk or move your body in some way. *Emotions need motion*, and a little movement goes a long way.

Emotional authenticity is a liberating value because it challenges the white supremacist cultural values of urgency and objectivity. It also makes room for a diversity of cultural expressions and communication styles.

#6. Release Expert Status

Being a leader, especially *the* leader, can create a bit of an ego trip. It feels good to be in charge, the ultimate decision maker, the go-to person, the expert in the room. It feels good to be the one people look to for advice, direction, and guidance.

However, if you are currently leading in a context where the status quo is not diverse, inclusive, or liberating, then your invitation is to release expert status. You're invited to submit to the leadership of those who know the way to a more liberating future.

This shift from "expert, leader" to "beginner, follower" may be personally costly to you, especially if you've been affirmed and groomed for leadership your entire life. If you are used to environments catering to you, it creates a rude awakening when you are no longer the one who holds the answers. If you've benefited from systems of oppression, you can't lead to liberation. You can follow, and you can practice embodying the values of liberation, but you cannot be in charge.

Practicing liberation will require you to release expert status. You have to embrace a degree of self-doubt. You have to suspend unquestioned confidence in your leadership instincts, especially if those instincts have been primarily formed within a privileged social location.

· · ● · ● · ●· ·

Practicing liberation will require you to release expert status.

· · ● · ● · ●· ·

Do It: Release Expert Status

- Attend anti-racism workshops or trainings in person and experience the discomfort of not being the leader in the room.
- Assume you do not know what's best and ask for help.

- Resist the temptation to correct or adjust the people on your team when they simply lead or go about tasks differently than you.
- When inviting content providers to teach you and your team about race, racism, and diversity, do not ask them to tone down their message. Learn from others as they are.
- Consistently find ways to follow the leadership and guidance of Black women and activists in real time. (Quick example: If you hesitated to say "Black Lives Matter" in 2015, but said it quickly in 2020, know that you were late to the work. As such, what are activists asking you to do now, in this moment? Do those things, even if they pull you out of your comfort zone.)

Releasing expert status is a value of liberating cultures, because it resists the white supremacist cultural value of paternalism. It also invites a great role reversal, wherein those who have been historically marginalized *lead*, and those who've been historically privileged *follow*.

#7. Grief and Lament

Our broad social culture prizes positivity, triumphalism, and good vibes. We are conditioned to believe feelings like sadness, despair, and anger are to be avoided at all costs. We don't have much space for heartbreak, lament, and grief. If we are experiencing those things, we've been taught to navigate those waters privately and alone. Few of us know how to sit in the shadowy places with one another. Few of us know how to acknowledge our rage or express our sadness. There is a very real pressure to "fix it" and to do it quickly. When optimism is the standard, we push through because "we've got work to do."

One of the most frustrating, and recurring, Black-girl-on-an-all-white-team experiences I've had is being told to "find hope." It's offensive when people who have never experienced the trauma, exhaustion, and centuries-old legacy of racism tell me to be hopeful. It's one thing when a fellow Black person, especially an elder, an auntie or grandmother, tells me to find hope. They are not talking from a place of their discomfort with my rage. They are talking from a deep well of love and experience. When Dr. Martin Luther King Jr. or civil rights legend John Lewis called Black people to hope, it was from the agony of bloodstained streets where they fought tooth and nail for freedom. It was not from the comfort and high horse of power and privilege.

When someone who has never experienced racism tells me to be hopeful, I've learned it has very little to do with me and everything to do with their discomfort with the reality of racism and systemic oppression. I get it. You don't want to believe things are as bad as they actually are. What we miss, however, is when we jump to "hope" without walking through the valley of the shadow of death, our hope is anemic. It does not serve marginalized communities. At best, it's a salve to ease our conscience. Cheap hope, a hope that costs nothing, does not set us free.

If we are to create liberating organizational cultures, spaces where our teams are empowered and equipped to participate in the reimagining of society, we must befriend our grief. We must practice lament. We must resist the temptation to feel better too quickly. And we most certainly must stop telling people to be hopeful when we have not lived through the pain and loss of their experience.

Do It: Grief and Lament

- Evaluate your personal comfort level with shadowy emotions, like sadness, despair, and anger.
- When racial crises strike, personally or across society, hold moments of silence for your team.
- Create a budget line item to cover the cost of therapy for your team members, especially those experiencing racialized trauma and harm.
- Grand social problems will not be completely resolved in our lifetime. Embrace the painful powerlessness of this fact.
- Follow the leadership of communities of color who have been advocating for their liberation for centuries. They are teaching us all what real hope looks like.

Grief and lament are liberating values because they make space for the fullness of our humanity. They also validate the painful experiences of oppression that people of color and other marginalized groups experience on a regular basis.

#8. Centering Marginalized People

Those most impacted by a problem are the ones who best know how to solve that problem. They are the experts. They have the best observations, experiences, and perspectives on the issues at hand. Those who've been excluded have the keenest awareness of what is needed to make inclusion real.

When you center marginalized perspectives, you are challenged to embrace "diversity of thought" on a whole new level. Just because two people share a racial identity doesn't mean they think the same things. No community is a monolith. Oftentimes, however, while we create space for White people to be fully individuated and unique, we tend to assume all Black people or all Asian people or all Latino/a people are the same.

What would it look like to center the experiences of those who've have been excluded from access to power, leadership, and influence in your organization and to do it in a dignifying way? Honoring the rich diversity of our humanity?

Yes, it will lead to more cooks in the kitchen. Yes, it will take longer to make decisions. Yes, building consensus may feel like things are getting worse before they get better. But this is the work of inclusion. It's always been more efficient to have a few decision makers and to gloss over everyone else. Centering marginalized people requires a new way of being. White supremacy culture says, "We don't have time for this." Liberation culture says, "We can't move forward without this."

Do It: Centering Marginalized People

- Don't make decisions about people when they aren't able to participate in those decisions.
- Find and read memoirs. You don't have to be friends with people from backgrounds unlike your own to learn about their experiences.
- Create safe opportunities for minorities (racial minorities, ethnic minorities, gender minorities, etc.) to give real feedback about what it's like to be on your team.
- When you hear difficult stories from marginalized people in your midst, believe them.
- If there are people from various minority groups in your organization who have taken on an informal "diversity leadership" role, pay them. Seriously. It's extra work. It's burdensome work. Dignify their labor by paying them for it.

Centering marginalized people is a liberating value because it amplifies the diversity, creativity, and leadership found in historically marginalized groups and communities.

#9. Reparations

Truth be told, I feel woefully underqualified to write about reparations in a substantial way. I haven't studied economics and, while I know a good bit of history, I can't recall all the details at the drop of a hat. Here is what I do know: if we are going to create liberating cultures, we have to commit to repairing harm. It's not enough to feel bad. It's not enough to apologize. Repairing harm is about doing what it takes to make things right, often at some level of cost to the one who has inflicted harm.

Many brilliant people have made the case for large-scale economic reparations for Black people. Ta-Nehisi Coates and Nikole Hannah Jones[4] are two voices that come to mind. For the average person, while you may have the privilege of electing public officials and advocating for the policies you value, you probably won't have the final say in whether or not the United States will pay reparations to those who've been exploited over time. But you do have the opportunity to take responsibility for how your privileges create barriers for others. You also have the opportunity, in moments where you cause harm, to own up to it quickly and publicly.

Do It: Reparations

- Research the case for economic reparations in the United States.
- Create a reparations fund or budget line item. When you or someone on your team does something harmful, create a process for paying the person who's been harmed.
  Note: You don't get to decide what is considered harmful or not. It's not about your intentions. It's about your impact.
  Note #2: This is not charity. This is a dignifying act of justice.

- When you say or do the wrong thing, own up to it quickly.
- When you say or do the wrong thing publicly, own up to it quickly and publicly.
- Choose practice over perfection here. It's not a science; it's an ongoing, highly relational journey.

Reparations are a value of a liberating culture because they are tangible ways to right the wrongs of history, on a macro and micro scale. Since perfection is not possible, reparations are an opportunity to resist an oppressive status quo and to imagine a new way forward.

#10. Imagination

Without the power of imagination, we cannot envision a different past, present, and future. What we cannot imagine, we cannot live into and struggle for.

—Kwok Pui-lan, theologian, author,
*Postcolonial Imagination and
Feminist Theology*

What would it look like for your team to reflect the demographics of the community you serve? What would it look like for your board of directors to be filled with the young and the old, the rich and the poor, men and women, and people from various racial and ethnic backgrounds? What would it look like for you to no longer be the boss or the leader, and for you to lend your gifts and energy to invest in the visionary work of someone unlike you?

Answering all these questions requires an imagination. It requires the courage to go back in time and re-learn history. It requires an honest and difficult confrontation with our current social realities and origin stories. It requires collaboration, creativity, and the tenacity to pave pathways to a new future. You have to envision radically different futures for your work, your team, and the institutions you lead.

Do It: Imagination

- Capture one of the values from this list and take five minutes to journal about what it could look like for you to consistently embody the value.
- Grab a stack of sticky notes (alone or with your team) and take sixty seconds to generate as many answers as you can to this question: For our company, what would a liberating culture feel like?
- Set a seemingly outlandish goal to reach for your team's representational diversity. What would have to change to make that goal a reality?
- Find one or two organizations whose expression of diversity, reconciliation, and liberation you admire. Interview a person on their team to see how they got there.
- Find a blank piece of paper and sketch what you hope the future of your organization, and its impact, is like.

Imagination is a value of a liberating culture because it challenges the status quo of every system of oppression you've been told is "just the way it is." Imagination is fundamentally empowering and generative. Imagination reminds us that anything is possible.

Take Inventory

Take a moment to assess which of these values you already see at work in your leadership and organization.

Fill out the checkboxes below.

Value	Within Me	Within My Organization
Embodiment		
Sharing Power		
Practice over Perfection		
Accountability		
Emotional Authenticity		
Release Expert Status		
Grief and Lament		
Centering Marginalized People		
Reparations		
Imagination		

For the sake of transparency, here is how I would fill in this box for myself and the organization I'm part of at the time of this writing.

Value	Within Me	Within My Organization
Embodiment	X	x
Sharing Power		
Practice over Perfection	X	x
Accountability		
Emotional Authenticity	X	
Release Expert Status		
Grief and Lament	X	
Centering Marginalized People	X	x
Reparations		
Imagination		x

As is the case for any culture and set of values, many of these values are overlapping and interconnected. For example, there are strong ties between embodiment and emotional authenticity. Organizationally, there is a strong connection between accountability and reparations.

Do you have to be a person of color to put these values to work? No. This work, though different for each person, is available to everyone.

Do you need a racially diverse team to put these values to work? No. At least not at first. You can do the work internally to cultivate an inclusive and dignifying culture before different kinds of people even arrive.

● ● ●

Contextualizing These Values

Let's revisit the stories from chapter one (the conference, the neighborhood protest, and the interaction with my mentor) and consider how employing these new, more liberating values may have changed outcomes. This exercise, in and of itself, is one of imagination.

The Conference. Outcomes for the conference could have been different if there was *shared power.*

The goal of sharing power is to create environments where different kinds of people are able to make decisions, craft messaging, share ideas, and effect change. Sharing power equalizes opportunities for influence. In the case of this event, sharing power could have looked like:

- Hosting the event with a partner organization, where responsibilities for event design and content curation were shared.
- Opening up the schedule to allot more time for the leaders of color to share their expertise individually, as opposed to folding all of them into one panel.

Sharing power is not about appearing diverse and politically correct. Sharing power happens when you believe in collective impact. Sharing power is an expression of need for one another's voices, perspectives, and gifts. Sharing power affirms that we're better together.

The Neighborhood Protest. In the case of the neighborhood protest, *accountability* could have made their advocacy work even stronger.

Accountability, a system of checks and balances, holds people up to the standard of continuing to work for justice, even when the problem is no longer in the headlines. Accountability asks, "What's next? What does progress look like? How do we course correct and stay engaged when pursuing liberation is no longer the cool thing to do?"

For a neighborhood community wanting to be proactive about racial justice, accountability could look like:

- Setting a specific area to work for racial justice for at least one year. The area could be housing legislation, police brutality, or the local education system, for example.
- Finding a partner organization working to solve a specific racial injustice and joining them (following, not leading).
- Establishing a weekly, bi-weekly, or monthly rhythm of convening to build momentum toward working for racial justice.
- Being open to feedback when confronted about the ways privilege deters well-intentioned people from staying the course.

The Interaction with My Mentor. The most helpful and liberating values my mentor could have embodied are *centering marginalized perspectives* and *releasing expert status.*

Had he put these two values to work, his posture toward my anti-racism efforts would have carried less, "Do this my way because your way won't make you successful . . ." and more, "We need your perspective and voice. Thank you for communicating so honestly. Tell me more. What do you see?"

This shift would have been personally beneficial to me. It would have also established a norm of valuing, instead of fearing, various marginalized perspectives. Creating space for a diversity of voices to flourish, as well as for honest feedback about racism to be heard and addressed, goes a long way in creating a diverse organization.[5]

NEW VALUES, NEW CULTURE

Pursuing racial and ethnic diversity and adopting new, more liberating values is fundamentally human work. It is messy. Anyone who tells you its formulaic, linear, and purely knowledge-driven is lying. Practicing the values of a liberating culture, especially as organizations and teams, is about real people, real stories, real values, real politics, real pain, and real possibilities.

This work is about people. It's about creating environments where dignity is affirmed and humanity is celebrated.

Ultimately, you have to adopt new, more liberating values and behaviors if you want diverse groups of people to flourish as they follow you. Systemic oppression is reinforced by societal and organizational culture. Practicing new values is one of the best ways to disrupt systemic oppression and the harm it causes. Do not underestimate the importance of putting new values to work in your leadership. Embrace cultural change.

DIVERSIFY
YOUR LIFE

- *Insight:* Your ability to cultivate a diverse personal life is directly tied to your ability to lead a diverse team.

- *Action:* Resist racism and pursue diversity in every area of your life.

A TALE OF TWO
LEADERSHIP CULTURES

It was my first day conducting research for a new project on organizational culture and diversity. In preparation, I'd confirmed two interviews: a morning focus group with two Black women who worked for an international development nonprofit, and an afternoon interview with a Black woman who worked for an architectural firm.

I arrived at a corporate office in downtown Atlanta for the focus group. As I struggled to find parking, the massive size of the organization became apparent. The cynical side of me was thinking: *How could an institution with hundreds of employees manage to get anything right about creating a diverse and liberating culture? It's too many people to keep up with!*

I made my way into the building, checked in at the front desk, and settled into a conference room for our conversation. I pulled out my recorder and notebook. Once the interviewees arrived, we got to work.

I started with a few softball questions, covering topics like, "Who are you?" "What do you do here?" "What do you love about your job?" As the conversation flowed, we turned to discussions about diversity, systemic injustice, and more. Due to the nature of their work (international development), their team regularly discussed issues of access, power, and storytelling. The interviewees pulled no punches as they shared about gaps in diverse representation at the board and executive leadership level. They also spoke transparently about the power games involved in managing the organization's diversity and inclusion strategy.

As the conversation rounded its final corner, I asked more explicitly about their daily experiences of belonging, engagement, and team culture. This is where they caught me off-guard. Despite the many organizational challenges their nonprofit was facing related to large-scale racial equity and diversity, at the end of most days, they left the office feeling heard, uplifted, seen, and supported.

These are the exact words they used.

Heard.

Uplifted.

Seen.

Supported.

I was both delighted and stunned.

One of the women went so far as to say, "Because I can be myself here, I can bring my best to the rest of the work I do."

Our conversation came to a close, and they helped me find my way back to the parking garage. As we parted ways, I thought to myself: *Maybe the problem isn't as bad as I think it is. Maybe most organizations are further along in their racial diversity and liberation work than I realized.*

A few hours later, I held my afternoon interview.

This interview was with a Black woman who worked for an all-white, and all-male, architecture firm. I followed the same line of questions from my morning conversation, moving from small talk to questions of diversity strategy throughout her firm, and finally to personal questions about her daily work experience.

Over the course of our interview, she sounded drained, hopeless, and defeated.

I posed my second-to-last question: "Can you be yourself at work?"

Her answer was decisive and clear.

"No. Not at all. And I say that quite emphatically. It doesn't cause me stress or anything. It's so ingrained now, the code-switching."

She paused for a moment, and then continued on:

"I'm naturally a leader with a very dominant personality. But I don't want to be seen as an aggressive Black person. So, I can't be myself. As a woman, I have to make things sound like a suggestion rather than a direct order. I always have to play this mediator role between conflicting parties. It's frustrating. Never being able to be myself. Never being able to share with my coworkers, especially if something race-related is happening in the news. I have no Black coworkers, because the firm is so small. I'm the only woman and the only Black person. It can become exhausting and mentally draining."

Her words hit me right in the chest. Especially the "mentally draining" part. It's one thing to simply go to a stressful job every day. It's a different experience to go to work and do your job, while also navigating a cultural environment clearly not designed for you.

I took a deep breath and asked my final question, "Do you think various diversity gaps can be closed in your industry?"

She replied, "No, not without major, major changes."

The Impact of an Intentional Leader

As I reviewed my notes, I analyzed the two scenarios. What factors led to such drastically different work experiences, especially where racial diversity was involved?

These three women had a ton in common. They were not only college educated, they had advanced degrees. Each, at different points in the conversation, referred to having loving personal networks of family and friends. They all had at least five years of experience in their respective fields. They found their way to their industries by following their passions and skill sets. In different ways, they each invested a great deal of time, energy, and money into advancing their careers.

However, when it came down to their daily experiences of workplace empowerment and inclusion, they had very different stories to tell.

While analyzing the transcripts, there was a significant finding. The two women I interviewed in the morning kept tying their positive workplace experiences back to one person: their supervisor. They spoke time and time again of this incredible person, a woman who did not share their racial identity (she was a White woman), but who'd gone above and beyond to create a culture where inclusion and racial diversity were the norm. They talked about how she understood her own racial identity, how she'd worked hard to know the effects of systemic oppression on all her team members (people of color and non-people of color alike), and how she leveraged her position to advocate for change through the organization.

I was inspired. Who knew a leader could make such a difference? Who knew a bit of intentionality could go such a long way?

Intentional leaders are people who take personal responsibility for creating liberating cultures. They hold themselves accountable to the work of finding and closing diversity gaps in their personal lives and leadership. They educate themselves. They find mentors to pave the way. They don't outsource "organizational diversity work" to consultants and the human resources department, believing they've checked it off the list. They believe practicing liberation on a personal level is integral to their formation as leaders and to the good work of their organization. They create safe and empowering places for team members to grow, learn, and lead. They have their own driving values for pursuing racial, ethnic, and cultural diversity. They invest in the journey, whether others are watching or not.

Intentional leaders confront racism, practice liberation, and create cultures where diverse groups of people can thrive. They are committed, even while working in large organizations that are difficult and slow to change.

To close the diversity gap and to create an inclusive organization, the first person you must teach to practice liberation is yourself.

LEARNING TO LEAD OURSELVES

Each of us carries a sphere of influence. Whether you are leading yourself, a family, or an entire team, you have the opportunity to be more intentional about the culture you're creating.

There are five areas where each of us has the chance to lead ourselves in a more liberating direction. As you read, consider one area of focus to concentrate on for a year. Doing so will change the trajectory of your life and leadership.

The five areas include:

- **You**, the leader
- **Your vision** for creating a diverse and liberating culture

- **Your people**, the ones you follow and the ones who follow you
- **Your places**, where you spend your time
- **Your stories**, the ones you inherit and the ones you choose

You, the Leader

Intentional leaders of racially diverse and liberating cultures embody at least three realities: racial and ethnic self-awareness, a growing understanding of systems of oppression, and a commitment to the ongoing process of change.

Racial and Ethnic Self-awareness

When you begin the work of pursuing racial and ethnic diversity, it is tempting to reach outward in an effort to understand the experiences of those who are unlike you. By reading books, listening to podcasts, watching movies, and asking questions, you learn a great deal about others. This is a good thing. However, when you focus exclusively on getting to know "the racial other," you miss the essential work of knowing your racial self.

One of the best ways to get to know your racial self is to return to your origin story. Begin with asking questions about how your family and community of origin shaped your racial worldviews.

In a racialized society, every person, regardless of racial and ethnic background, carries racialized thoughts about the world and about people. We internalize perspectives on who should lead and who should follow, who is dominant and who is subordinate, who is trustworthy and who is not trustworthy, and so on.

Increasing your racial and ethnic self-awareness begins with interrogating the racial perspectives you bring into any given room. Ask yourself questions like, "Who did my parents teach me to trust based on race?" "Who did they teach me not to trust?" and, "What stories about people from different racial groups did I learn from my grandparents, based on what they said or didn't say?" Your racial and ethnic origin story is impacting your leadership today.

Increasing your racial and ethnic self-awareness also invites you to learn more about the privilege you have experienced based on your identity and social location. As your racial self-awareness grows, you are better equipped to relate cross-culturally in dignifying, nonexploitative ways. Being aware of who you are enables you to make generous space for others and the unique gifts and perspectives they bring to your organization.

Understanding Systems of Oppression

During my focus group with the two Black women from the international nonprofit, I wanted a deeper glimpse into exactly what this supervisor did to make them feel "heard, uplifted, seen, and supported." I asked for a story to illustrate this point, and one of the women spoke up:

> One expression of white supremacy in our organization is most of the people of color who work

here are in lower-level positions. When it's time for layoffs or restructuring, the people of color are often the first ones out the door, even if they deserve to be here. Our supervisor understands this dynamic, and in an effort to maintain job security for the racial and ethnic minorities in our organization, she reserves a portion of her annual budget to hold positions for racially diverse talent who may lose their jobs when other departments do a purge. This is how I've been able to work here. She got to know me when I worked for another department, and when that department laid me off, she hired me because she believed in what I brought to the table.

When I heard this story, I was blown away. This supervisor understood the nuances and complexities of systemic oppression—systems that create advantage for some and barriers for others. Because she understood the system of white supremacy, she proactively created a scenario where those who experience the most barriers in light of white supremacy could keep their jobs.

I'm sure she wasn't able to preserve employment for everyone, but she preserved it for a few. This leader's proactivity also created a scenario in which her organization's stated value for diversity was put into practice. She did this without a grand organizational overhaul.

Intentional leaders are always working to understand and apply liberating interventions to systems of oppression. This kind of understanding doesn't happen overnight. It takes years of thoughtfulness, growth, and creativity. But it is possible.

What would it look like to discover which system of oppression is most prominently hindering your racial, ethnic, and cultural diversity goals? What would it take for you to confront that system head-on?

Commitment to the Process

Crisis moments will come and go. Internal and external pressure to change will also come and go. Depending on your experience of privilege, you will always have the opportunity to opt out of leading your organization in a more diverse and liberating direction.

You decide. And, ultimately, the only person who can truly hold you accountable to the long journey of this work is *you*.

There are two major shifts you have to make if you want to influence your culture in a new direction. You must shift from reaction to responsibility, and from avoidance to leadership.

I recently revisited the *Lord of the Rings* trilogy. It's one of my favorite stories. As I've found my own voice and responsibility as a leader, the story arch of Aragorn's character has been meaningful.

For those who are unfamiliar with the story, Aragorn, a main character in the narrative, was born in the bloodline of a king. However, due to the failings of kings before him, he decided to abdicate his responsibility to the throne. He spent years on the fringes until time and circumstances forced him to make a decision about his future. He could continue to avoid responsibility, or he could decide to take his rightful place as king of Gondor.

Aragorn was afraid of leading because he didn't want to screw it up. But his avoidance didn't serve anyone, not even himself. He had to make the choice to lead.

The same decision rests with you. No, you're not waging a war for the soul of Middle-earth, but you are tasked with creating culture and with empowering the people you lead.

You can no longer settle for reactive diversity trainings and fearful avoidance of hard realities.

You get to bravely choose a more liberating way.

This work begins with the leader. This work begins with you.

Key Questions

What were you taught to believe about race and racism?

How are these lessons and beliefs impacting your leadership today?

Your Vision

Imagination is a value of liberating cultures. Your task is to leverage imagination in order to identify your unique vision for pursing racial and ethnic diversity. Why are you compelled to engage in this kind of work? What is motivating you? What do you want to see changed in your leadership, organization, and community?

Imagine a different future. Imagine your organization filled with people from all kinds of backgrounds. Imagine the creativity and innovation flowing. Imagine your ability to respond meaningfully to social injustice. Imagine a culture where you're able to serve your clients more effectively because your team represents the varied and valued perspectives of your customer. Imagine open feedback loops for effective, even if difficult, conversations. Imagine authenticity and true community.

Intentional leaders make time to envision a new future. Their vision goes beyond diverse representation. They imagine a reality where every person is seen, respected, heard, and able to contribute in significant ways.

The goal of this imaginative exercise is to discover an authentic vision for racial and ethnic diversity, one that resonates with who you truly are. As your vision emerges, write it down, share it with others, and invite a diverse group of collaborators to make the vision better and clearer. Once you and a team of collaborators have a picture of where you're headed, let others know. Tell them why. People who follow you need to know why you're making a change. Sharing a purposeful vision empowers others to decide how to engage. It also creates a chance for people to opt out if pursuing diversity, resisting racism and white supremacy, and embodying more liberating values doesn't align with their vision.

If you fail to communicate the *why* for the change, you not only miss out on engaged participation, you also create an environment where silent resistance to change can fester. Communicating the vision gives you the chance to rally those who are on board and to decide how to engage with those who are not.

Key Questions

Why is racial, ethnic, and cultural diversity important to you?

Why is equity, inclusion, justice, and anti-racism work important to you?

Why do you want to practice liberation?

Your People

Practicing liberation impacts every person who interacts with your organization. You can start by thinking about this work in terms of your team, executive leadership, and board of directors. But the opportunity for organizational cultural change extends to other groups as well, including, but not limited to:

- Investors
- Donors
- Contractors
- Volunteers
- Clients
- Social media followers
- Partner organizations

When you think about pursuing greater racial and ethnic diversity in your organization, ask yourself: "Who am I following?" and, "Who is following me?" This includes social media, but it's not limited to interactions online. The people in your life have a profound impact on how you see the world.

Organizationally, it may be worthwhile to focus your diversity efforts on one branch of the organization at a time. What would it look like to spend twelve to eighteen months focusing on racially and ethnically diversifying your donor base? How would you confront racism and white supremacy to pursue a new kind of donor community?

Or perhaps you want to tap into new volunteer communities. Doing this well requires building trusted inroads to organizations beyond your current network. How might you do this in a dignifying and reciprocal way?

Building meaningful, mutually beneficial relationships with new groups of people is an important next step in your personal liberation practice. These sorts of connections are cultivated over meals and through shared experiences and honest conversations.

Key Questions

Write a list of the key stakeholders involved in your organization's operations.
With which groups do you want to focus your diversity efforts and why?

Your Places

Proximity matters. Where you spend your time determines whom you know.

In my interview with Dr. Michael Emerson,[1] a sociologist and professor in Chicago, Illinois, we talked extensively about the role of *place* in our efforts to build racially diverse communities. We specifically discussed how the historical segregation of cities throughout the United States continues to create barriers to building meaningful cross-racial connections.

Dr. Emerson first realized he lived in an "all-white" world one year while reviewing his holiday card mailing list. Every person and family on the list was White. In response, he turned this into a research question. Through a series of indexes, he learned that he lived in one of the whitest communities in the United States. After this realization, along with a series of other lessons related to systemic racism and injustice, he and his family changed everything. They moved to a nonwhite neighborhood, began attending a nonwhite church, and he enrolled his children into schools where they, as White children, were the racial minority.

Choosing where you live, where you work, or where you set up your company's offices are significant personal decisions. It's important to remember, however, that this highly personal decision doesn't unfold in a vacuum. This decision has implications for the kind of city you live in, the networks you create, and much, much more.

Where you spend your time determines who you know. And who you know often determines how you see and interpret the world.

I asked Dr. Emerson what the average person can do when he or she lives in a racially homogenous community (e.g., when where you live, work, attend school, practice worship, and so on, is composed of one racial group). His recommendation is to look at all the places where you spend your time and select two places to change.

In asking Dr. Emerson about the impact these shifts had on his family, he explained how his now-adult children are not only thankful for their upbringing, but they feel better equipped to lead meaningful lives of impact because of their experiences of racial and socioeconomic diversity as children.

The decision to physically move your life is filled with challenges and opportunities. Adopting cultural humility, increasing your self-awareness, and continuing to pursue liberation are all essential practices if you choose to relocate.

Key Questions

Where in your day-to-day life do you experience authentic connections to people who are racially and ethnically unlike you?

What two places can you change to lead more of a racially heterogeneous life?

Your Stories

The stories you are immersed in shape everything about who you are. There are the origin stories you inherited from your family and the community you grew up in. There are the stories you believe unconsciously. There are the stories you pursue and consume through media (social media, movies, the news, etc.). And there are the new stories you choose to listen to and believe.

Pursuing diversity, resisting racism and white supremacy, and practicing liberating values in your life and leadership come back to two consistent activities: 1. interrogating the stories you were given (as discussed in chapter one), and 2. integrating new stories you encounter and choose to believe.

You get to decide which new stories you want to carry into your future.

Maybe you heard a podcast or read a memoir, and it challenged your worldview. Maybe you received feedback from a team member, and it made you reevaluate an aspect of your leadership. Maybe you spent time immersed in a community unlike your own, and you've discovered entirely new insights on life and leadership.

New stories are found everywhere. When you begin integrating these new stories, you position yourself to lead with self-awareness and empathy.

We get to choose new stories, and new stories can change the world.

• • ● • •

We get to choose new stories, and new stories can change the world.

• • ● • •

A MOMENT FOR QUESTIONS
AND RESPONSES

Below is a series of frequently asked questions people have related to creating a more diverse personal life and resisting racism and white supremacy on a personal level.

What do I do when confronted with an internal bias of which I was previously unaware?

As you move forward, you will see layers of internalized bias at work underneath the surface of your life. This may be disorienting or shame-inducing. Shame often drives us into hiding, or toward suppressing a difficult truth you've discovered. To combat the temptation to go into hiding with this new information, you have to drag it into the light. You have to confess it. You have to tell the truth.

One way to do this is to write it in a journal. After writing it down, interrogate the bias, asking questions like, "Where did this bias come from?" or "Who or what taught me this?" After self-reflection, find a safe person with whom to share this bias. Ideally, this person is a friend, trusted counselor, or advisor. The goal in sharing is to keep you from getting stuck in a shame cycle. It also empowers you to choose a new story moving forward.

I've heard a lot about the impact of implicit bias in organizational diversity work. How can we know our implicit biases if they are truly unconscious?

Great question! There are countless experts on implicit bias out there who could speak to this way better than I can. In my experience, my body always reveals the truth about what I think or feel about others. Whether it's a tightness in my chest, an uneasiness in my gut, or a negative thought on repeat in my mind. My body tells the truth.

Pay attention to your body and to how you respond when interacting with different kinds of people and in different kinds of spaces. Note your reflexes. Pay attention to the ways you're inclined to respond (leaning in, pulling away, etc.). Noticing your body's responses will give you rich data on the biases and preferences you experience with different kinds of people.

How can I start integrating new stories into how I see the world without asking others to share their personal stories of harm with me?

There are many options. There are podcasts, movies, books, and blogs. There are many people who share their stories of race and identity online, in print, and beyond. It can be overwhelming to find the right learning medium, but that is part of your work.

Look for and listen to all kinds of voices on race and diversity. Cast a wide net. You will love some aspects of what you find and dislike others. That's okay. It's also part of the work. When listening to podcasts or reading memoirs, listen for when the creators of the content share their own recommendations for voices to follow. You can start anywhere. As long as you're curious and open-minded, you will find new stories. If you let them, those stories will change your life.

This work makes me so emotional. Anger, shame, and fear seem to rule the day. How do I get out of these emotional spirals and actually do something constructive?

Emotional health and wellness are essential. You don't have to be perfect, but you do need to be self-aware. Why? Because confronting racism, practicing liberation, and closing diversity gaps is personal work. It challenges who you believe yourself to be. There are power dynamics, family baggage, racial trauma, and all kinds of doubts and insecurities present.

If you are experiencing a degree of anger, shame, or fear related to this work, then you're human. These emotions are data. They are also invitations for you to seek out the support you need to be well. Remember your humanity; be patient with yourself. If it is accessible to you, go to therapy. And connect meaningfully with other people who are on this journey.

My world is all white, and I want to start changing that without being seen as strange or off-putting. How do I find new places to build diverse community without being awkward?

There may not be a way to do this without feeling awkward. You're deciding to go against the grain of your socialization, after all. Discomfort is the name of the game.

But discomfort is a powerful teacher. "The right to comfort" is one of the highest values of white supremacy culture. To create a new culture—for yourself, your team, or even your family—you'll have to give up your right to be comfortable at all times. Building connections to new people in new places is a vulnerable and uncomfortable action. But a little humility and consistency will take you a long way.

The more I learn, the more I see how I've caused unintentional harm to others over the course of my leadership journey. What do I do about this?

You are not alone. We are all learning and unlearning. The more we know, the broader our perspective becomes. It makes sense that, as you look back over your leadership, you see areas where you wish you'd known better and done better.

As best you can, forgive yourself. Where possible, repair the harm. You can do this by redistributing your resources or by apologizing. If appropriate, you can ask the harmed party what you can do to make it right. In your efforts to repair harm, make it about the other person, and not about assuaging your guilt. It may take some creativity, but repair is worth pursuing. Ultimately, all you can do is your best.

LEAD WITH COURAGE

- *Insight:* People don't just want a job; people want to belong. Your intentionality and vulnerability set the tone for how much belonging is possible.

- *Action:* Lead with vulnerability and courage.

BUILDING FOR BELONGING

I was gearing up for my first summer away from home. I was nineteen years old and made plans to live on the westside of Chicago with a group of eight other college students. Our objectives for the summer were simple: get to know our neighbors and volunteer for the neighborhood youth camp. Interestingly, however, the most transformative aspect of this summer was not the new neighborhood or volunteer work.

The most transformative aspect of the summer was learning how to live and work with a diverse group of eight strangers.

Here are a few types of diversity reflected in our group:

- **Racial and ethnic diversity**—there were three Black people, one Asian person, and five White people.
- **Regional diversity**—one of us was from the South (me), a couple were from the Northeast, and a few were from the Midwest.
- **Academic diversity**—we represented small liberal arts schools, elite private schools, and large public universities.
- **Religious diversity**—we all came from the same faith tradition, but participated in very different expressions of our collective tradition.
- **Socioeconomic diversity**—some of us came from wealthy families, some of us from low-income families, and others of us were somewhere in between.

We also had varying degrees of exposure to worldviews other than our own.

In a normal workplace situation, these differences may take years to surface, if they surface at all. For our group, however, it was only a matter of days. We did everything together: volunteering, grocery shopping, cooking, eating, and exploring the city.

Thankfully, as differences emerged, we were prepared to navigate them.

At the beginning of the summer, our group leader taught us the four stages of community new groups experience when moving from stranger-hood to belonging. Coined by American psychiatrist M. Scott Peck,[1] the four stages include:

1. Pseudo-community
2. Chaos
3. Emptying
4. True community

(1) Pseudo-community: This refers to the surface-level interaction and relationships experienced when first getting to know new people. In this phase, time is focused on avoiding conflict and on emphasizing what people have in common with one another. Differences are minimized to encourage group conformity and togetherness.

(2) Chaos: Eventually, differences emerge, conflict is felt, and each stranger in the group is faced with a choice to either retreat to pseudo-community or go deeper into relationships, even though it's difficult.

(3) Emptying: For those who choose to move through the chaos, emptying is the most important stage of all. This is where members of the group disclose more of who they are and work through the tensions hindering effective communication. In the emptying stage, group members dive into differences, work through the challenges of being differentiated human beings, and build connection through honesty.

(4) True community: On the other side of emptying, people begin to experience true belonging. Group members begin to

embrace the fullness of one another—the good and the not-so-good. Marked by authenticity and depth, true community is where each person gets to be themselves.

The stages of community illuminate the process of building a diverse team. While research suggests diverse teams outperform homogenous teams,[2] this is only possible when diverse groups of people know how to work together without compromising individuality. Moving from the surface, through the chaos, to a place of authenticity is the journey of any team seeking to experience true belonging.

People experience belonging when diversity is cultivated, racism and white supremacy are resisted, and liberating cultural values are practiced at the organizational level.

WHAT IS BELONGING?

There are as many definitions of belonging as there are people. Each person experiences the gift of being accepted, wanted, and embraced in different ways. However, there are three characteristics of belonging consistently found across time, communities, relationships, and organizations: authentic presence, brave communication, and radical inclusivity.

Authentic presence is the experience of bringing your genuine self into every environment, because you're secure in who you are. While this sense of security must be cultivated internally, as a leader, you can create an environment where authentic presence is validated. Pay attention to what uniquely energizes your team members. Celebrate them when they use their gifts. Affirm distinct perspectives. Regularly ask for their input and put their ideas into practice. Give people leeway to take risks and to test out new ideas. When people speak up on uncomfortable topics, listen well and thank them for sharing. These are a few ways you can validate the authentic presence of others on your team.

Brave communication happens when you tell the truth of your experiences and listen to the truth of others' experiences, especially related to matters of identity. This communication requires bravery because it is vulnerable. As a leader, you set the tone for brave communication in your organization. Directly confront issues of racism and white supremacy in your work environment. Initiate important conversations. Express appreciation when team members share difficult feedback or divergent ideas. Own up to your mistakes. These actions set the tone for brave communication.

Radical inclusivity is the ongoing practice of removing barriers to participation for historically marginalized or oppressed groups of people. Throughout this book, you have learned about racism and white supremacy, and how practicing liberation can begin removing barriers for people of color. There are many other barriers to remove as well, including barriers that exclude women, people with disabilities, LGBTQIA+ people, and working parents. As a leader who aspires to create a liberating culture where people can experience belonging, finding and removing these barriers is your work to do.

● ● ●

WHEN BELONGING IS THREATENED

As you translate ideas from this book into your daily efforts to lead others, there are a few points of tension to monitor. These points of tension are tipping points. They will either propel you into greater racial, ethnic, and cultural diversity, or they can cause your work to fall apart. The tipping points are power dynamics, trust, relational clarity, and repeated interactions.

Power Dynamics

Increasing racial, ethnic, and cultural diversity without redistributing power among racial groups can cause more harm than good, especially when people of color primarily fill entry-level positions (as opposed to having diverse racial representation across all levels of the organization). In these scenarios, lower-level employees rarely have the organizational influence required to address negative impacts of marginalization in the work environment.

Increasing diverse representation at every level in the organization is one way to begin practicing liberation on an organizational level. You can also practice liberation by mapping the kinds of power you personally carry as a leader and finding creative ways to give power away.

While power comes in all shapes and sizes, here are four kinds of power to pay attention to:

1. Decision-making power: who makes the most decisions or who makes the decisions impacting the greatest number of people.

2. Money-related power: who makes the most money or who decides how much money everyone makes.
3. General influence: whose opinion carries the most weight or who decides which opinions matter most.
4. Voice-related power: who talks the most or whose words and ideas shape the organization the most.

It may be your job to manage these aspects of your organization. As you move forward, consider how you can share power within these responsibilities for the sake of closing diversity gaps.

You can create internal committees tasked with making key decisions for the whole organization. You can build a team of employees who weigh in on the creation of compensation packages. You can make your communications team more collaborative to increase the diversity of voices shaping your messaging. These are all ways to redistribute and balance power.

Trust

Trust is difficult to come by when it comes to race. Racial division is historical and deeply entrenched into every aspect of culture. Most team-building activities are ill-equipped to dissolve centuries-old racial and ethnic strife.

This presents a challenge for teams who want to practice liberation on an organizational level. Even with your best intentions, the choice to build bridges across lines of racial difference lies with each individual on your team. You can create environments for learning, regularly confront racism, write polices to practice liberation, and more. You cannot, however, change people's minds. People change their own minds if and when they want to.

As a leader, when the inability to build trust becomes a tipping point for your organization's ability to close its diversity gaps, your only option is to tell the truth.

Tell the truth about your racial origin story and experience. Tell the story of how your eyes have been opened and your worldview changed. Tell the truth about mistakes you've made and risks you've taken to repair harm. Trust is built when the truth is told; be honest about your story.

Writer and teacher Parker Palmer says, "Truth-telling by a leader can legitimate truth-telling at every level."[3] Being honest about your shortcomings, about the shortcomings of your organization, and about how you sincerely want to do better will encourage others to do the same.

Relational Clarity

When bringing together a team, you may be tempted to use the language of family to create a sense of belonging. This is a nice sentiment, but it must be used thoughtfully. Being a team is not the same as being a family. Families don't have job descriptions, salary packages, team meetings, performance reviews, legal checkups, and so on. You can't fire your family.

Workplace belonging is one experience; family is another.

When family language is used in the organizational context, you lose relational clarity. All sorts of working dynamics get out of whack. Using family language makes accountability difficult. It generates false expectations of unconditional acceptance. Boundaries between life and work get blurry, and it's tough to know which hat to wear in any given interaction.

Am I the boss or the friend?
Am I the employee or the little sister?
Am I going to be fired?
Is it okay if I quit?

Here is a personal example to illustrate the confusion family language can create on a team.

I once had a supervisor who flip-flopped between behaving like my boss and behaving like my friend. When interacting with him in any given moment, I didn't know which version was in the meeting. This generated anxiety. In one moment, our interactions felt friendly and light. On those days, the power distance between us would shrink, and we'd relate as equals. On other days, he'd be wearing the supervisor hat, the power distance returned, and he'd give orders and direction.

In moments where I needed to give him difficult feedback related to work or the organization, he would jump into "friend" mode, encouraging me to trust him and let it all go. By jumping out of the "boss" box, even momentarily, he avoided responsibility for the impact of his organizational leadership. However, when he needed to give *me* difficult feedback, he'd *put on* the boss hat again, leveraging the influence of his position to compel me to change a given behavior. As my boss, he used his position to encourage my compliance, which is something a friend would not and could not do.

Familial language is a tipping point because it not only creates relational ambiguity, it also assumes every person has a positive and similar understanding of what it means to be a family. It's not true.

Rather than using family language to create a false sense of belonging, work with the members of your organization to determine what belonging actually means in your context. Resist the temptation to project what creates belonging for you onto the people you lead. This takes time. You have to listen, learn, take notes, and hold many conversations. You have to clearly articulate the values, practices, habits, and policies that make belonging possible for the people on your team. Using family language is a shortcut. At its worst, it's manipulative and causes trauma, especially for those who experience any degree of harm in your workplace.

Repeated Interactions

Every organization has containers for its internal operations. These containers include team meetings, supervisor or manager 1-on-1's, performance reviews, informal gatherings, and public events. Each of these environments is an opportunity for the gap between your good intentions and your impact to get larger or to get smaller. This ultimately hinges on your ability to create positive and inclusive interactions for the people on your team when they experience repeated interactions in your organization.[4]

Here are a few insights to monitor as you work to create a liberating organizational culture.

In Team Meetings

- Who sets the agenda? Is it the same person every time? Is there a way to make the agenda creation more collaborative? Smaller organizations can crowdsource agenda items from various team members. This way, anyone can bring up a topic or priority for the larger group to discuss.
- Who talks the most and who talks the least? Pay attention to who feels enough confidence and belonging to share their ideas in a group setting. Pay attention to who does not. You may not need to fix anything right away, but this data will help you determine whom your culture supports the most and whom it supports the least.

*In Supervisor or Manager
One-on-Ones with Employees*

How racially and ethnically self-aware are your supervisors and managers? How nuanced is their understanding of systemic realities impacting their team members? If supervisors are not doing their part to understand their racial identity, their power, and their privilege (or the lack thereof), they will be ill-equipped to connect cross-racially and cross-culturally with their supervisees. Monitor how people are experiencing these one-on-one connection points with the people who manage them.

In Performance Reviews
with Team Members

A good friend of mine, a woman of color, once refused to attend her final performance review as part of a majority white organization. The review was slated to be part exit interview and part performance review on a presentation she'd recently given. She had been the only Black woman on the team for years. She was leaving the organization for many reasons, some of which were related to the racial (and racist) dynamics at play.

Her manager, another friend of mine, could not understand why she would not participate in this conversation. He is a White man and an executive-level leader on this team.

When he and I connected to discuss this, I told him: "She doesn't feel safe attending this review because she can't trust that your feedback will be accurate. She can't know if what you're saying is bias against her because she's a Black woman, or if what you're saying is true about her performance. For this time to be effective, she'll need someone else in the room who can help her parse out what is true and what is your racial bias against her."

He understood and went on to bring in a mediator who could hold space for both of their perspectives. She felt honored and psychologically safe, and he was able to fulfill his duties as a supervisor.

When it comes to simple activities, like performance reviews, it is impossible to check all your biases and your distinct cultural perspective at the door. You bring them with you into every conversation, meeting, and leadership decision. The goal isn't to become free of all biases. It is impossible to do so. The goal is to become aware of your biases and to adjust your processes to serve the people you lead.

In Informal Gatherings

Fun activities and informal gatherings go a long way in creating culture. If your hope is to create informal gatherings that are fun *and* inclusive, here are a few questions to ask:

Is your entire planning committee from the same social location (e.g., the same race, same gender, same socioeconomic status, etc.)?

If so, it's possible you're creating a socially exclusive experience where those who are unlike you will have to assimilate, code-switch, and, therefore, have less fun.

Is what you're planning financially accessible or inaccessible? Will everyone on your team be able to participate or will cost hinder the participation of some? What can you do about this?

A quick fix would be to cover all expenses for everyone who participates.

Is what you're planning actually fun for everyone, or is it uniquely fun to a particular cultural group?

If you find it's only fun to one cultural group, you don't have to necessarily change your activity. Be mindful that what's fun for you may not be fun for others. Next time, choose an activity others would enjoy, especially if it gets you out of your comfort zone.

YOU SET THE TONE
FOR BELONGING

Each day, your leadership sets the tone for how much belonging is possible. This happens through the stories you amplify and the ones you silence, the heroes you celebrate and the people you villainize, the truth you tell and the secrets you hide. Each of these actions has an impact on who experiences belonging in your organization.

• • ● ● • •

Each day, your leadership sets the tone for how much belonging is possible.

• • ● ● • •

When you choose to be honest, to course correct when threats to belonging emerge, and to share vulnerably about your racial awareness journey, you are closing the diversity gap. You are creating a culture where all people are seen, heard, respected, valued, and able to contribute in meaningful ways.

Lead with courage. Keep going.

A MOMENT FOR QUESTIONS AND RESPONSES

Below is a series of frequently asked questions people have related to creating a more diverse team, practicing liberation, and resisting racism and white supremacy on an organizational level.

How do I diversify my team without tokenizing people?

In an interview, author and entrepreneur Sam Collier said, "If you hire one or two people of color and you don't have plans to hire more, you're in tokenism. If you hire one or two minorities and you *do* have plans to hire more, that's not tokenism; that's the beginning of something new."[5]

The tension around tokenism has to do with the critical mass of people of color who are being recruited to diversify a majority-white team. Diversity and inclusion expert Janet Stovall says, "Thirty percent is critical mass, when minority groups can actually start to be heard."[6]

The question lies with you: Are you interested in hiring enough non-White people to make your team appear more diverse, or are you hiring enough people of color to fundamentally change the culture of your organization?

Tokenism makes room for the one. Liberation makes room for the many.

I am White, and I supervise people from all kinds of racial and ethnic backgrounds. Any tips on how I can do this well?

If you are a White person and you are leading, mentoring, coaching, or managing non-White people: (1) Find ways to be mentored by people of color, either in person or via resources they share (books, podcasts, etc.); (2) Cultivate self-awareness; and (3) If and when you hear stories about racism from the people of color you're leading, listen and believe them. Do not try to fix, diminish, or explain them away. Listen well. If you say anything, let it be these three words, *"Tell me more."* Your job in those moments is to be a container for the experience of another, and if you carry it well, you'll build trust. If you don't, you'll break trust. These moments are incredibly important.

I am a person of color, and I supervise people from all kinds of racial backgrounds. However, my biggest challenges are with the White people on my team. They don't respect my leadership. Any thoughts on how to navigate this?

Be yourself and do your job with excellence. It's challenging to convince people who don't respect people of color, or women, that they should. If the relationship is toxic and unhealthy—in other words, filled with blatant disrespect and lack of regard for your humanity and leadership—invite colleagues into the conversation to help you find your best next step. If you wait for people to respect you, or if you bend over backward to vie for others' approval, it will cost you more than you'll gain.

8

NEW LEADERS, NEW FUTURES

- *Insight:* No one is asking you to be perfect. We are asking you to get uncomfortable, be creative, take some risks, and show up with consistency.

- *Action:* Do your work.

NEW LEADERS, NEW FUTURES

We're in a moment of immense cultural change. Long-held beliefs and ways of operating are being questioned, dismantled, and reimagined. This ambiguity is enlivening for some and daunting for others.

While it can be exciting to face a blank slate of creativity, it's difficult to start from scratch.

While it's energizing to imagine what *could* be, it takes time to translate the vision into reality.

Change is also filled with loss; we lose our stability, our illusions of control, and, in some instances, our very sense of self. Pursuing liberation and creating new cultures means saying goodbye to old, familiar structures and ideals. There is grief. There are layers of surrender and countless emotions along the way.

Despite the challenges, creating the cultures of the future is work worth doing. It's worth it to learn how exclusion, racism, and white supremacy have caused harm. It's worth it to discover a more liberating way.

Why?

Because lives are at stake. Because the well-being of people is on the line. Because, as a leader, you are in the business of creating environments for the growth and development of others. The onus is on you to disrupt harmful patterns and to invest resources in cultivating the best possible workplace conditions for others.

You are invited to become a new kind of leader, one who pairs good intentions for diversity with true cultural change.

New kinds of leaders emerge in three ways.

#1. Seasoned Leaders Get Immersed in New Communities

If you've held leadership positions in majority white institutions for many years, you've been formed to lead in ways that maintain the status quo of those institutions. This is normal. However, to pair your good intentions for diversity with cultural change, you have to be formed in a new way. This formation happens through traditional learning, but it happens best in community.

What would it look like to immerse yourself in a context where you must follow the leadership styles, habits, and practices of those who've experienced the harm of oppression? When you position yourself as the follower and trust the instincts of leaders who know oppression firsthand, your leadership instincts are disrupted. You learn there are multiple ways to accomplish a goal. You learn there are multiple styles, values, and priorities related to leading others. If you're a seasoned leader, one of the challenges you'll confront in this immersive experience is the temptation to still be in charge. Resist it. Learn how to participate fully in a community where you are not the leader. Do this and you'll be on your way to closing your diversity gaps.

#2. New Leaders Find Their Voices in Communities of Practice

If you have not been in leadership positions for many years, and yet you have a vision for how to create a more liberating and inclusive culture, what would it look like for you to start leading? What would it take for you to speak up, gather others, create community, and inspire change? Learning how to lead also requires community.

My friends and mentors Donna and Leroy Barber founded a nonprofit organization called The Voices Project. Its mission is to train and promote leaders of color. In a conversation, Donna talked about the importance of community in helping underrepresented people find their voice. Many people of color who have worked or volunteered in majority white institutions for multiple years struggle to know what their authentic voices sound like. Because of this, people of color (and other underrepresented minorities) don't always know how to speak up when the time comes. Donna and Leroy create communities where leaders of color can come together to talk about issues they care about, the struggles they are facing, and their ideas for how to make the world better. In this affinity space, emerging leaders of color find their voices and are equipped to return to majority white spaces with confidence.

Does this sound like the kind of community you need to start your leadership journey? We all need a safe place to find our voices, learn our unique leadership styles, and discover our own liberating practice. What would it look like to gather a few others who are on a similar journey and find your voices together?

#3. Finding New Leaders in Surprising Places

Beyond the walls of our organizations, there are teenagers, immigrants, refugees, activists, farmers, and artists who are all challenging us and inviting us to imagine a more liberating way forward. The question is not: Are there people who are leading us toward liberation? The question is: Are we willing to follow the marginalized, the outcast, or the unexpected people who are showing us the way?

There are countless people in the world who are imagining new kinds of organizations, businesses, and ways to lead.

They are pairing their good intentions with action. There are young people advocating for Earth justice. There are Indigenous communities fighting for sovereignty and sustainable relationships with the land. There are activists taking to the streets, holding our democracy up to its highest ideals. There are elders teaching us what it means to hold on to hope. There are immigrants starting businesses and creating communities. There are refugees risking everything to make a better home for their families. There are resilient, everyday folks who will never give TED talks or see their names on book covers. These, too, are people worth following. Worth listening to. Worth believing in.

Open your eyes to the teachers all around you. Let them lead you. Trust them to show you how to put action to your good intentions for change.

THE INTERSECTION OF INSIGHT AND ACTION

Closing the gap between our good intentions for diversity and true cultural change is only possible at the intersection of *insight* and *action*. Insight is about what you see and know. Action is about what you do in light of what you know.

• • ● • • •

Action is about what you do in light of what you know.

• • ● • • •

The insights shared in this book aim to reframe how you think about diversifying your organization. The key insights are:

- Racism and white supremacy are the root problems. They must be continually addressed and resisted as you pursue diversity.
- Your impact on people of color is more important than your good intentions.
- Your motivation for pursuing diversity has implications for how harmful or helpful your diversity strategies will be.
- There are multiple frameworks through which to engage the work of diversity, and you have to know which framework you're operating in at which time.
- Embrace new, more liberating values in order to create a culture where diverse groups of people can flourish.
- Pursue diversity, resist racism and white supremacy, and practice liberation on a personal level if you hope to do it on an organizational level.
- The people who work for you want to experience belonging. You set the tone for how much belonging is possible.
- You do not need to be perfect. You do have to get uncomfortable, be creative, take some risks, and show up with consistency.

Each insight, to be effective, is paired with an action. The actions are:

- Take inventory of how racism and white supremacy exist within your culture. Adjust your diversity strategy to disrupt these systems.
- Prioritize hearing, believing, and following people of color.
- If your pursuit of racial diversity is about dignifying people and disrupting racism, keep going. If this is about appearing relevant, stop.
- Choose your framework for pursuing diversity and know why.
- Practice liberation; embody cultural change.
- Resist racism and pursue diversity in every area of your life.
- Lead with vulnerability and courage.
- Do your work. Pair your good intentions for diversity with actual cultural changes.

When you regularly gain new insight, and act differently in light of what you've learned, you are on your way to closing the diversity gap.

Four Possibilities

The intersection of *insight* and *action* creates four possibilities for your organizational culture (see Figure 4).

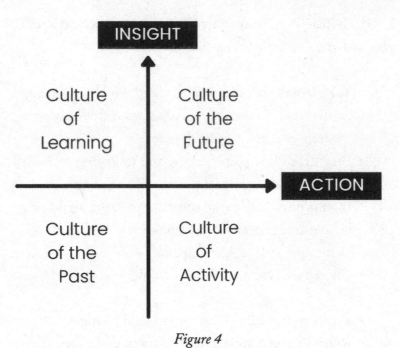

Figure 4

The insight-axis refers to your ever-evolving under-standing of racism and white supremacy, and their impact on your organization, your leadership, and society as a whole. It also refers to how well you understand your role in upholding or disrupting racism and white supremacy. As you learn more about these systems and their impact, you move from low-to-high on the insight-axis.

The action-axis refers to the activities you do, the resources you allocate, and the experiments you try in an effort to create a more diverse and liberating culture. This includes hosting workshops, working with consultants, facilitating dialogues, creating learning opportunities, having difficult conversations, being self-reflective, donating money to liberating causes, and joining protests. As you put your energy, body, and resources to work, you move from low-to-high on the action-axis.

At any given moment, you are creating:

> *A culture of the past* (low in insight, low in action)
> *A culture of learning* (high in insight, low in action)
> *A culture of activity* (high in action, low in insight)
> *A culture of the future* (high in insight, high in action)

Cultures of the Past

When an organization is low in *insight* and low in *action*, it is perpetuating a culture of the past. These cultures tend to be homogenous, insulated, and self-serving. As society moves toward greater racial and ethnic diversity in every sector, cultures of the past double down on old ways of doing, thinking, and leading. This is the opposite of innovation.

If you find yourself, or your team, in this quadrant, movement will happen when you can no longer afford to stay the same. It may not seem like it at first, but there is a cost to not changing. In a society increasingly committed to pursuing racial equity, a vote to stay the same is a vote to fall behind. Not only might you lose business, clients, and partnerships, but you'll be ill equipped to outperform more racially and ethnically diverse teams who have done the work to cultivate authenticity and belonging.

Cultures of Learning

Cultures of learning are marked by acquiring information, finding stories, and sharing ideas. In these organizations, people are continually growing in their understanding of systems of oppression. These cultures have a high value for unconscious bias trainings and diversity workshops.

As someone who loves ideas, I thrive in cultures of learning. And yet, knowing more information doesn't necessarily lend itself to practicing liberation and dignifying people. Action involves changing how we live and lead. It hinges on using our bodies and our voices for the work of increasing diversity, resisting racism and white supremacy, and practicing liberating values. Cultures of learning are important. This is a phase every organization must go through for their action to be effective. Learning alone, however, is insufficient to make an organizational culture more freeing and affirming for all people involved.

Cultures of Activity

When activity and movement are consistently prioritized over gaining new insights and reflection, a culture of activity is at work. Imagine being on a team where there is an outburst of disconnected and unrelated efforts toward diversifying the organization. There are committees being formed and book clubs being started. Diversity statements are drafted and protests are attended. Lots of activity for the cause of increasing diversity and addressing racial tensions!

And yet, moments of reflection are few and far between. In cultures of activity, people rarely take time to step back and look at the big picture. The work to increase diversity and address racism is short-lived in these organizations because leaders have not paused long enough to truly understand and solve the root problems at hand.

There are seasons where activity must be prioritized. In moments of racial crisis and injustice, we must be quick to move toward action. We can't, however, remain in a state of constant action. It's unsustainable and can lead to personal, and organizational, burnout.

Cultures of the Future

Cultures of the future are environments where leaders are committed to expanding their insights and engaging in meaningful actions. It's a dance; it requires rhythmic movement between the two, integrating moments of learning and moments of activity into the organizational calendar.

There are rhythms for every aspect of working life. There are seasons for on-time and off-time. There are times for fundraising and spending. There are moments set aside to focus on marketing, invest in the sales funnel, and for the professional development of team members.

To create a culture of the future, you must build structures for the change you want to see. Keep an eye out for when you are stuck in "learning" mode, "activity" mode, or "maintaining the status quo of the past" mode.

If you are in a culture of learning—good! Keep learning. As you learn, find ways to apply new insights. How might you mobilize your physical body, your resources, or your time to shift your culture toward the liberating practices of the future?

If you are in a culture of activity—great! Keep acting. As you act, set aside specific times to reflect. Ask yourself these questions: Of all our activities, what has made the greatest positive impact? What has led to little or no impact? What new insights do we need to move forward?

If you find yourself in a culture of the past, choose to either expand your insights through learning or to increase your action through new activities. By increasing one or the other, you shift your culture in significant ways.

LEADERS OF THE FUTURE

For leaders who aspire to pursue organizational diversity, to resist racism and white supremacy, and to create the liberating cultures of the future, there are ten characteristics to prioritize:

#1. Leaders of the future are peacemakers, not peacekeepers.

Peacekeeping is reactive. It's self-preserving, silent in the face of injustice, and pulls away from challenging relationships and conversations. Peacekeeping protects the status quo.

Peacemaking, however, is proactive. It anticipates challenges and adjusts course for the sake of the common good. Peacemaking is characterized by humility and truth telling. It disrupts the status quo for the sake of liberation. Peacemaking actively builds bridges to others, even when the outcome is unknown.

#2. Leaders of the future make themselves accountable.

It takes trust and humility to tell someone who works for you, "If I cause harm in any way, let me know." Furthermore, it takes tremendous self-control to receive feedback when someone tells you, "Hey, you did this, and here's how it was harmful to me."

Leaders of the future make themselves accountable to others. They open themselves up to feedback from the people they lead. The vulnerability can be excruciating. There will be times when the feedback is not even accurate, and yet, making yourself accountable creates an environment where change is possible. It also creates an environment where historically silenced voices can be heard and validated.

#3. Leaders of the future think collectively and individually.

While the individual is often elevated as the most significant unit in Western society, leaders of the future know the individual is only healthy and well if the collective is healthy and well. The "collective" is inclusive of you, those who are like you, and those who are unlike you.

Leaders of the future think beyond individual achievement and growth. They are always wondering, "Who are we and how are we? What needs to change for the collective to thrive?"

#4. Leaders of the future are relentlessly self-aware.

Leaders of the future are committed to knowing themselves. They know their strengths and their weaknesses. They know their hang-ups and their breakthroughs. To be a leader of the future, you must be on a journey of learning who you authentically are. What origin stories inform who you are, who you value, and whose stories matter to you? Why are you interested in diversifying your team or practicing liberation? What inclines you to give up on confronting racism? What motivates you to keep going?

The best leaders have answers to these questions, and they are invested in answering these questions over the course of a lifetime.

#5. Leaders of the future are truth tellers.

Sojourner Truth once said, "Truth is powerful and it prevails."[1] Leaders of the future tell the truth. They communicate honestly. They initiate difficult but clarifying conversations. They own their part in causing harm, and they tell the truth about how they've experienced harm.

Leaders of the future create environments where the truth can be told responsibly, but without punishment or retaliation.

#6. Leaders of the future filter everything through the lens of liberation.

Leaders of the future filter all organizational realities through the liberation framework. Practicing liberation spans beyond the representation of who is on your team. It encompasses legal decisions, financial processes, hiring pipelines, compensation packages, and board leadership. As a leader of the future, you may not be able to change every aspect of your organization, but you can ask the question, "What role, if any, are racism or white supremacy playing in this aspect of our work? What do we want to do about it? What would it take to practice liberation in this area?"

Asking new questions will lead to new answers; new answers lead to transformation and liberation.

#7. Leaders of the future clarify language.

What do you mean when you say "diversity"? What does it mean to pursue "inclusion," "equity," "liberation," or "justice"? Words matter. Leaders of the future are intentional about the language they use to shape the culture of the organizations they lead. There is a learning curve here; you have to know your options to identify the right words for your team or community.

Leaders of the future do the work to know their options and move forward with conviction.

#8. Leaders of the future decenter themselves to prioritize another's point of view.

One of the most challenging aspects of leadership is being misunderstood. People misunderstand your motives, your stories, your personality, and your work.

Leaders of the future are not immune to the negative impacts of being misunderstood. But leaders of the future practice decentering themselves long enough to prioritize the needs and experiences of others.

#9. Leaders of the future embrace clumsy conversations.

We often want our conversations on race, identity, and systemic oppression to be easy. Up and to the right. Simple. Clear. To the point. That is not how it works. Conversations on these topics are messy, cyclical, highly personal, and they unfold imperfectly over time.

Leaders of the future embrace the clumsiness of this work. They hold space for their own imperfection, and the imperfection of others, in the process.

#10. Leaders of the future take risks to create the cultures they say they want.

The most important work of our lives requires everything but guarantees nothing. Consider parenting. As a parent, you invest countless hours of energy and tons of money in the cultivation of this little life. And yet, you have very little control over who your child decides to become. Diversity and liberation work are similar. You give time, energy, and resources to efforts you hope will make a difference. But you can never know for sure.

Leaders of the future take bold risks to see their good intentions become good impact for all people.

YOU HAVE WHAT IT TAKES

You are creating the organizational cultures of the future. By your actions, or your inactions, you are deciding what the future of your workplace will be. You are deciding whether your organization will uphold racism and white supremacy or dismantle them. You are creating a culture, and it will shape generations to come.

This is a profound responsibility. It's not lost on me how fundamentally disorienting it may be to question your origin stories, center new perspectives, and commit to making real changes in your organization. Despite the difficulty, you have what it takes to become a new kind of leader. With authenticity, consistency, and courage, you have what you need to chart a new course for the workplaces and organizations of tomorrow.

• • ● • • •

You have what it takes to become a new kind of leader.

• • ● • • •

THE JOURNEY CONTINUES

Closing diversity gaps in our lives, leadership, and workplaces is an ongoing journey. As is the case in any journey, there are ups and downs, twists and turns, hopes and disappointments.

Much like life itself, you never arrive. You simply commit. You keep moving forward. As you've worked through the ideas, frameworks, and stories on these pages, I hope you have found the direction you need to take your next best step. Our culture is in desperate need of people who will lead with integrity and courage. May you be one such leader.

And may your very best intentions for diversity lead to true culture change.

ACKNOWLEDGMENTS

I was told by many how challenging it is to write a book. They were telling the truth! This has been no easy feat, and I have so many people to thank for their support along the way. Thank you to the following:

Alex: for honoring the creative time and space I needed to bring this book, and so many other projects, to life. I love you.

My family: for always believing in me and my wildest dreams. I know anything is possible because of you.

Courtnee Wilson, Jhana Crabtree, Keonnie Igwe, Jazzy Johnson, Pamela Barba, Ines McBryde, Caroline Lancaster, and Kaitlin Ho Givens: for holding space for me, in all my Blackness and woman-ness, as I've journeyed toward greater liberation.

Kayla Stagnaro and Jeff Shinabarger: for cheering me on in every season and for believing in this book when it was just a one-page Google Doc.

Brooke Powers: for keeping *The Diversity Gap* podcast running and for using your stellar operational skills to keep me sane.

Lydia Mays, Deshawn Adams, Ale Trevino, J'Tanya Idiodi, and Tiffany Johnson: for reading the first, and very messy, drafts of my book. Your time, thoughtfulness, and curiosity made this book better.

Chris Ferebee: for being my agent and walking with me through every step of this publishing journey. Your presence has been such a gift.

Tim Burgard, and the team at HarperCollins: for seeing the message I wanted to share with world, believing in it, and taking a chance on a newbie author.

Plywood Women's Layers: for holding me down through all the twists and turns of leading an authentic professional life.

Plywood People: for believing in *The Diversity Gap* podcast and research project, and for being the kind of community where dreamers can make their ideas a reality.

And finally, to The Diversity Gap community: for sharing your wisdom on *The Diversity Gap* podcast, for sharing your stories in interviews and focus groups, and for leveraging your influence to spread the message of good impact far and wide. I'm endlessly grateful for you!

Appendix A

DIVERSITY TO LIBERATION FRAMEWORK

AN ASSESSMENT

To complete the assessment, read through each of the fifteen statements, one at a time, and circle the response that resonates with you the most. After you have circled one response to complete each statement, you will go through each column and tally the number of circles in that column.

		Column A	Column B	Column C
1	When the topic of diversity comes up at work, my priority is . . .	Articulating how our efforts will directly address racism and white supremacy	Making space for people to talk honestly about their hopes and fears	Identifying a specific outcome and building a strategy to reach it

		Column A	Column B	Column C
2	The problem(s) that keep(s) me up at night is/ are . . .	White supremacy, the patriarchy, Christian hegemony, settler colonialism, etc.	Wondering how to make sure everyone feels safe, equipped, and prepared to have the tough conversations	Not knowing which intervention will have the greatest return on investment
3	My go-to solution for diversity challenges is . . .	Activism and holding leadership accountable to make a difference	Learning more about one another's histories and cultural backgrounds	Recruiting and hiring people from varied backgrounds to diversify our team
4	It's difficult for me to understand the importance of . . .	Making sure our marketing materials reflect diversity	Creating a dashboard to measure and track progress	Talking about racism and white supremacy all the time
5	I get frustrated with others when they focus on . . .	Talking about the issues instead of doing something about them	The tactical interventions instead of the relational dynamics	Systemic issues and relational dynamics instead of measurable change
6	The guides I trust to lead us toward progress are . . .	Activists and Black women!	Facilitators, historians, and teachers	Consultants and organizational change strategists

		Column A	Column B	Column C
7	My biggest fear in pursuing this work is . . .	The possibility that we can't reform the old; we can only build the new	We'll break trust with each other and no longer be able to work together	We'll spend a lot of money on new solutions, but our organization will stay the same
8	Success looks like . . .	Aligning our activity to serve the most marginalized	Talking about identity and culture with confidence and respect	Improving the racial/ethnic makeup of our team by x percent
9	I wish my team members would focus on . . .	Addressing their internalized white supremacy	Listening to one another and really understanding where every person is coming from	Expanding their networks to recruit more diverse candidates
10	I feel stuck when we disregard . . .	The voices of those most impacted by the problems	The impact race-related conversations are having on everyone	The importance of measuring progress
11	I celebrate . . .	Policy change and representation at the highest levels of leadership	Effective conversation across race, especially when there's been conflict	Public-facing communications (social media, websites, events, etc.) representing the diversity we're working toward

		Column A	Column B	Column C
12	Our organization will be stronger when . . .	We align with movements for radical change	Our cross-racial relationships are authentic, safe, and full of respect	Our team internally reflects the face of diversity we share externally
13	I want to help my team to . . .	Create systems of accountability	Create spaces for hard conversations	Stay focused on the task of diversifying our leadership and staff
14	My responsibility in leading this work is . . .	Sustaining pressure on those leading to confront systemic issues	Ensuring every person has a voice	Finding the external consulting and coaches to keep us on track
15	I want our team to be known for . . .	Creating spaces where all people are truly free	Incredible community and a truly inclusive culture	Truly diverse representation at every level of leadership and engagement
	Tally:	_____	_____	_____

Tally your results.

If your highest tally is in Column A, you are mostly inclined toward the liberation frame.

If your highest tally is in Column B, you are mostly inclined toward the reconciliation frame.

If your highest tally is in Column C, you are mostly inclined toward the diversity frame.

Now that you know where your home base is, here are a few questions to consider:

- What encourages you about identifying your frame? What surprises you?
- Does your frame align with the frame of your team or organization? If so, how? If not, how do you know?
- Which frame would feel the riskiest for you to pursue? What is one vehicle from that frame you can engage in the near future?

Appendix B

QUESTIONS FOR REFLECTION AND DISCUSSION

Chapter One: Racism Is the Problem

- What is your origin story? Who are you and what stories from your life help you to know who you are?
- In this chapter, racism is defined as "a system of advantage and disadvantage based on race." How does this definition differ from what you were taught? How is this definition similar to what you were taught?
- Have you made plans to address and disrupt racism as part of your organizational diversity strategy? Why or why not?

Chapter Two: Impact over Intentions

- When are you most tempted to protect the origin story of your organization? What can you do to change this?

- Which story from this chapter surprised or challenged you the most? Why and what does that mean for the way(s) you lead?
- What would it take for you to create environments where BIPOC can do their best work without the ongoing distraction and burden of racism and white supremacy culture?

Chapter Three: Motivation Matters

- What if pursuing work in a dignifying and equitable way required you to step back from your current position? What if pursuing this work required you to step forward into a new position? How does the thought of making these shifts impact you?
- Which "case for diversity" has been most prominent in your organization's diversity work?
- Do you see any patterns of harmful diversity in your organization? What are they?

Chapter Four: Choose Your Framework

- Have you ever experienced burnout related to racial justice work? Why did it happen? How did you recover?
- What is your experience of the word "liberation"? In your own words, how does liberation differ from diversity, equity, and inclusion?
- Which frame—diversity, reconciliation, or liberation—is most comfortable for you? Which is least comfortable?

Chapter Five: Embrace Cultural Change

- Does navigating the dominant culture in the United States come easily to you, or is it difficult for you? If it's easy, how so? If it's difficult, how so?
- Which systems of oppression have you observed in your leadership context?
- Which values of a liberating culture come most naturally to you? Which seem most daunting?

Chapter Six: Diversify Your Life

- Have you ever experienced a great leader? What made that person stand out to you?
- Which of the five areas of intentionality are you going to focus on first?
- In this chapter, we discuss the importance of integrating new stories into our understanding of race, diversity, and liberation. What is one new story you've encountered recently that has shifted your thinking? Why did it impact you?

Chapter Seven: Lead with Courage

- Have you ever experienced true community and belonging? If so, what made it possible?
- Which of the four threats to belonging is most likely to undermine your organizational practice of liberation? Why? How can you address it?

- We each carry unique leadership skills and abilities. What is one superpower you bring to this work that equips you to create a liberating culture? (Share confidently! No half-brags allowed!)

Chapter Eight: New Leaders, New Futures

- Are you a seasoned leader in need of immersion into new communities or an emerging leader in search of your voice? How do you know, and what does that mean for you?
- Is your organizational culture a culture of the past, a culture of learning, a culture of activity, or a culture of the future? How do you know?
- Do you know any leaders of the future? What are they like? How has their leadership impacted you?

Appendix C

EXPERIMENTS AND STRATEGIES

C reating a diverse organization—and one equipped to proactively resist racism and white supremacy—is not a one-size-fits-all endeavor. You will have to discover a plan that works in your context.

This appendix will help you use your insights and actions from the book to find that plan.

This is a collection of experiments and strategies gathered from leaders, peers, and entrepreneurs pursuing organizational diversity in a variety of ways. They are categorized into the topical buckets and are listed in no particular order:

- Recruitment and Hiring
- Creating Learning Programs for Your Team
- Facilitating Dialogues and Conversations
- Personal Development
- Centering Marginalized People and Perspectives

- Strategic Planning
- Diversifying Your Board of Directors
- Advocacy and Justice

A couple disclaimers:

1. Even though many ideas are listed, I cannot definitively say which strategies would work best for you. I would have to know more about you, your story, and your context to create a comprehensive strategic plan.

2. Many of the ideas below are not fully fleshed out. They are *ideas*. The work of contextualizing, designing, and thoughtfully executing these ideas is on you and your team.

If you're interested in hands-on coaching, strategic planning, or facilitation, visit www.thediversitygapacademy.com.

RECRUITMENT AND HIRING

Give diversity a head start.

When there is a position to fill on a team, it's common practice to create a job description and shop it around to familiar networks in search of your next hire. This creates a challenge for creating diversity if your networks are racially, ethnically, and socioeconomically homogenous.

When you have an opening, go out of your way to push your job description into new networks. You can do this via social media, intentional outreach to new partners, and by listing your job descriptions on new job boards. Give this outreach a two- or three-week lead time before you share the description with your usual network. It takes time for applicants who are unfamiliar with your work and organization to get to know you and generate interest in applying. By giving diversity a head start, you're creating conditions where increasing racial, ethnic, and cultural diversity are possible. You're also setting yourself up to find excellent new candidates.

Emphasize credentials less and experience more.

Do your job descriptions list requirements that aren't truly integral to getting the job done? Do you require a four-year degree or a master's degree, even though the job could be done by a person with basic computer and communication skills? Unless you are looking to hire a doctor, teacher, lawyer, or a role requiring highly specific training, get creative.

Ask yourself: "Do I truly need a college graduate for this job? Or do I need someone who has multiple years' experience in the service industry? Do I need someone with X number of years in this industry, or could someone from an unexpected industry add value to my team?"

Lived experience is what prepares people to get the job done.

Pay your interns.

Offering unpaid internships, even if legal for nonprofit organizations, makes interning with your organization inaccessible for economically under-resourced people. In the context of the United States, those who are most likely to be economically under-resourced are people of color, specifically Black people, Indigenous people, and Latino/a people.

On a systemic level, offering unpaid internships advantages those who are financially resourced enough to work for free. They go on to list your organization on their résumé, while those who could not afford to work for free miss out on the professional development opportunity you've created. Offer paid internships, and see if and how it impacts the racial, ethnic, and socioeconomic diversity of your applicant pool.

CREATING LEARNING PROGRAMS FOR YOUR TEAM

Start with hopes and fears.

Once you've decided to engage the work of racial diversity and liberation from oppressive systems, create an opportunity for your team members to share their hopes and fears. This data can inform many aspects of your emerging program, including topics to focus on, groups to include, training that is needed, and the best pace of change for your organization. Depending on your organizational culture and how comfortable people are with self-disclosing, you can capture this information via an online survey, in a group meeting, in a one-on-one conversation, or written anonymously.

Listen to new stories, together, part one.

Driven by a desire to not only diversify their company, but also to create a culture where different kinds of people can thrive, the founders of Imagine Media Consulting created a three-month event series called "Perspectives." For this series, they invited (and paid!) a diverse set of entrepreneurs (in terms of race, ethnicity, sexual orientation, etc.) to share their stories of life, leadership, and identity with the entire consulting firm. This weekly lunchtime series was a low-stakes way for this team to begin having conversations about diversity and identity.

To make this work in your context, select four to six dates in your organization's calendar (these can happen, for example, weekly, every other week, or once a month). Curate a list of four to six speakers or storytellers. Determine how much you can pay them. Extend invitations, assign dates, send out calendar invites, and order lunch for the team.

Listen to new stories, together, part two.

Set aside a consistent meeting time (weekly, every other week, or monthly) and, for each meeting, assign one person in the group (or have people volunteer) to be the storyteller. Whoever is the storyteller for that session will tell his or her origin story, sharing about key people, ideas, and events. This is a very personal activity and should only happen where significant trust has been established. This should also be entirely voluntary; group members must opt in to this type of experience and commit to attending all the meetings. The ideal size for this group is four to six people.

Find another organization who cares about this work and join it.

You don't have to reinvent the wheel when it comes to hosting events and creating experiences for your team to engage topics of diversity, liberation, and justice. In many communities, there are multiple organizations who are exploring these exact topics. If you are out of your depth in creating new programming, find people hosting events nearby or online. Sign up, participate, and host a casual mealtime session to debrief what you learned.

Host trainings or workshops your team members can attend if they want to.

There are countless organizational trainings on diversity, anti-racism, implicit bias, and more. Some are incredible; others are not. Either way, it's important to make these training opportunities voluntary. When people are forced to attend trainings related to diversity and inclusion, it can create resentment. This resentment often turns into resistance to the diversity and liberation efforts at work within the organization. When people attend these trainings out of a desire to do so, it fuels the work. They take ownership in exciting ways. So, yes: hire the trainer and host the workshop. But don't force it or it's likely to backfire.

Another way to make trainings and workshops accessible is to encourage your team members to find trainings they want to experience and then pay for them to attend.

Hold a book club, movie-watching club, or podcast-listening club.

Informal, but consistent, media learning opportunities are a great way to encourage new kinds of conversations related to practicing liberation. You may run into hiccups if you mandate this (similar to the challenges of hosting mandatory training), but initiating a learning club or community can go a long way. It doesn't need to be an official workplace activity.

If reading a book is too much of an undertaking, consider curating a series of TEDx videos to watch, or gather a few podcasts to listen to. You've got options.

FACILITATING DIALOGUES AND CONVERSATIONS

Set ground rules or group agreements.

Meaningful conversations are integral to practicing liberation, both personally and organizationally. One of the best ways to make difficult discussions constructive is to establish ground rules, group norms, or group agreements at the beginning of the conversation.

Examples include:

- Use "I" statements, as in, "I think . . . ," "I feel . . . ," "I observed . . ."
- What is said in this room stays in this room.
- Acknowledge intent, attend to impact.
- Say "Oops" when you've made a mistake, and say "Ouch" when someone's comments cause you harm.

It's helpful to post your agreed-upon norms in the room where everyone can see them. This equips the group to self-monitor when people step outside of the norms and rules.

Use a quotation or poem to anchor the conversations.

There are times when people don't know how to start the conversation. As the group leader or facilitator, find a poem or quotation to anchor the conversation. Have the group read the poem or quotation aloud and ask people to share their thoughts or feelings about the piece. This takes the pressure off of you to have to bring all the content to the conversation. It's also refreshing to hear from a voice or perspective not present in the room.

This is a great exercise if you're in a homogenous group. Read a poem or quotation from someone who is unlike you and let it spark new thinking.

Use a timer.

A simple practice is to give each person the same amount of time to respond to a prompt or question. Some people will fill the time; others will not. Either way, it builds trust when the group knows time is being well managed.

Let silence linger.

Every moment in a dialogue need not be filled with noise. As you're facilitating groups, if it takes time for people to start speaking up and sharing their ideas, let the silence linger. Do not rush to fill every empty moment with more talking. People are often thinking or listening and need space to decide what to share.

Break up the discussion time.

When a prompt or question is given to the group, allot two minutes for quiet self-reflection and five minutes for sharing one-to-one with a partner. This gives people time to reflect personally, and to share in a lower-stakes scenario (for example, one-to-one) before opening the floor for large group sharing. Giving people multiple and varied ways to reflect and share honors the various personality types and communication styles of people in the room.

● ● ●

Hire a mediator.

Some conversations are best handled by an objective third party. When there are important, yet challenging, conversations on the table and you want to preserve the relationship, bringing in a third party will create psychological safety. It will also keep you and other involved parties focused on the task at hand.

PERSONAL DEVELOPMENT

Establish rhythms for focusing on diversity and liberation work.

Look at your calendar and choose a daily, weekly, monthly, quarterly, or annual rhythm to focus on a specific area of your organization. You can use this time to reflect, to learn something new, or to address a recurring challenge. Setting aside small, consistent blocks of time to focus on your personal liberation practice will make a difference in your leadership. Note: It can take twelve to eighteen months to see progress in one area of your organization. Set a rhythm to focus on one thing for twelve to eighteen months.

Meditate.

Diversity and liberation work can be challenging. Meditation is one way to decompress, to practice mindfulness, and to integrate self-compassion. Cultivating a meditation practice can help you stay grounded and equip you to lead from a place of purpose and ease. Three helpful meditation resources are the Headspace app, the Calm app, and the Liberate Meditation app.

Journal.

Journaling helps you increase self-awareness, work through challenging relationship dynamics, and gain new perspective on your experiences. Here are a few questions to guide your journaling practice:

1. When did you feel closest to others today?
2. When did you feel furthest away from others today?
3. When did you feel connected to something greater than yourself today?
4. When did you feel disconnected from something greater than yourself today?
5. When did you feel closest to yourself today?
6. When did you feel furthest away from yourself today?

By responding to these six questions on a consistent basis, you will discover patterns. You will find what drains you and what encourages you. You will see clearly what brings you joy and what fills you with dread. This exercise, and others like it, keep you on track toward increased self-awareness and emotional health.

Give your platform away, part one.

If your privilege has afforded you the resources, time, or opportunity to amass a large platform, especially digitally, give your platform to underrepresented, marginalized people or communities. Invite content creators from various backgrounds to "take over" your feed. This is not only a practice in decentering yourself, it also amplifies historically marginalized perspectives.

Give your platform away, part two.

When people invite you to speak at events, if their lineup doesn't reflect the racial, ethnic, and cultural diversity you claim to value, say *no* to the opportunity and make specific recommendations to the committee that invited you of historically underrepresented voices they could add instead.

Choose to move on from your position.

Depending on your social location, the time may come where you can't take the organization where it needs to go as it relates to diversity and liberation. If you are unable to remedy this by adding new people to the team you lead, it may be time to move on and make room for someone new. If moving on from your position permanently is not an option, consider stepping away for an extended season. This will create space for new leadership to emerge.

CENTERING MARGINALIZED
PEOPLE AND PERSPECTIVES

Create or support affinity groups or employee resource groups.

Affinity groups are intentional spaces created to support groups of people who have minority experiences within a majority culture. They exist to create room for encouragement, support, and professional development for people experiencing marginalization within an organization. Affinity groups can be based on race, gender, sexual orientation, parental status, and more. They vary in programming, size, and design. These groups can also support the larger organization in its cultural change efforts by recruiting from their personal networks or offering solutions to diversity-related challenges. There are many resources online related to launching these affinity spaces, also known as "employee resource groups."

If your team or organization isn't large enough to have affinity groups on its own, research if regional affinity groups exist for the communities you want to center and support.

Set aside additional funds for professional development.

When creating your budget for the upcoming year, double the professional development funds designated for people of color in your organization. Not only is this an acknowledgment of the harmful impact racist organizational cultures have on people of color, but it is also an act of care and respect. Additional resources can fund therapy, additional training, or other POC-initiated professional development opportunities.

Pay people of color if they are doing extra labor related to workplace diversity.

In an ideal world, employee work related to diversity and liberation would be demonstrated evenly among all team members involved. However, the work of diversifying the organization often rests on the shoulders of those it most impacts: the people of color. This is not inherently wrong if the people of color want to be leading this work. Even if they are fully opting in, it's extra work on top of their normal job description. If paying people who lead this work isn't a possibility, discuss this dynamic openly. What would it look like to offer tangible expressions of appreciation to those who are leading you on this journey?

Find a mentor who is unlike you.

You can begin centering marginalized perspectives in your own life by seeking out mentorship from people who are unlike you. Mentors get to weigh in on your leadership but don't have to navigate the power dynamics of working for you. You can be honest about your curiosities, and they can be honest in their feedback.

Do you need to pay this person to mentor you? Depends on what would be dignifying to the specific person you have in mind. If you want a relationship that is more structured and outcomes-driven, you might explore hiring a coach.

STRATEGIC PLANNING

Set one goal and create metrics around the goal.

Select one area to focus on over the next twelve to twenty-four months. Create metrics around that one goal and go for it.

An example: I was recently working with a nonprofit leadership team. They realized their donor community had less than 5 percent representation of people of color. Their team decided to focus the next twelve months on racially and ethnically diversifying their donor community, believing this would shape their racial diversity and liberation pursuits at every other organizational level.

What could your one-year goal be?

Hire a director of diversity.

Hiring a director of diversity can be a catalytic experience. Having a designated person who shows up to your office every day with an explicit focus on your organization's racial diversity work and liberation practice can be a game changer. This is especially helpful for larger organizations with complex and multilayered systems to consider. You will likely need someone to hold it all together.

If you're a smaller team, test this idea out by hiring a fractional diversity director or consultant. This person would have a smaller scope of work, and it would be a contracted position, which gives you flexibility.

Choose your words and decide what they mean for your organization.

> *Diversity? Equity? Inclusion? Belonging?*
> *Equality? Justice? Reconciliation?*
> *Multicultural? Multiethnic? Multiracial?*
> *Anti-racist? Anti-oppressive?*

What are your words? Why are those your words?

Choose words that move you to action. Choose words your team can support. Choose words you can define and embody. One way to find these words is to ask the people on your team which words resonate with them.

Language matters, but you don't need a PhD in critical race theory and organizational change to create a liberating culture. Don't let perfectionism and fears about language get in the way of doing the work.

Create a diversity dashboard.

A dashboard is a spreadsheet that clearly defines your goals and your progress toward those goals.

Here's what this could look like: Imagine you are the executive director of a large organization. This organization has twenty people on staff, four executive leaders, and nearly a thousand community participants. You have multiple content streams, team leaders, and communication pipelines, as well as a variety of operational focus areas. Here are the steps to take to create the dashboard:

Step One: Connect with each supervisor or team lead.

Step Two: Identify one diversity-related goal to focus on for one year.

Step Three: Answer the questions, "What does success look like in relation to this goal? How will we know we've reached it?"

Step Four: Write it down.

Step Five: Establish a rhythm to check in, ideally monthly.

Step Six: At each check-in, celebrate progress toward the goal and/or course correct.

Step Seven: Track this data in the spreadsheet.

Step Eight: Once the goal is met, celebrate.

Step Nine: Repeat the process, beginning with step one.

At the end of the year, look back to see where each team made progress and where each team struggled. Use this data to build future iterations of your strategy.

Create a cross-functional task force.

Gather a group of stakeholders from across the organization and empower them to lead your organization's racial diversity and liberation practice. This cross-functional team needs to have representation from every group of stakeholders involved in your operations. For a traditional nonprofit, this would include board members, staff or team members, donors, and clients or community members. For a for-profit entity, you may include investors or customers. By creating a cross-functional taskforce, you increase the likelihood of designing a diversity program that is integrated into your core functions and has buy-in from multiple stakeholders.

Map out your internal liberation team.

Build an internal team that is committed to prioritizing your organizational liberation efforts. This is different from the cross-functional taskforce, as this internal team is focused on the organization's internal culture and employee experience. This team needs to comprise the following roles and perspectives:

- The Diplomat—a person who can hold multiple interests and perspectives at one time
- The Critic—a person who can identify harmful systemic dynamics and is willing to explain these dynamics to the group
- The Guide—the person who knows where you're going and how to get there
- The Advocate—the person who is always looking for those who are not represented but should be
- The Champion—the person who challenges the group to keep going when it wants to quit

- The Timekeeper—the person who sets the rhythm, manages the calendar, and makes sure the meetings and events actually happen

Choosing who fills which roles is a group endeavor, and ought to consider personality (how are people wired) and giftedness (what are people good at).

Create a culture book.

A culture book is a physical or digital document for employees. It tells them who you are as an organization, the key stories defining your work, and the core values shaping organizational behavior. These documents are meant to be creative and thoughtful. Creating a culture book streamlines your vision for each person who joins your organization.

DIVERSIFYING YOUR BOARD OF DIRECTORS

Invite long-standing board members to retire their service.

One way to make room for new people, and new kinds of people, on your board is to invite long-standing board members to step down. How? Sit down with the individual, cast the vision for the future of the organization, and invite that person to step back and make room for new leaders. The beginning of this script could sound like this:

[Insert name here],

We are so thankful for your many years of service to this organization. You have helped us accomplish [x, y, and z]. As you know, we have been on a journey to racially diversify our organization and be more intentional about justice and liberation. One expression of this is diversifying our board. Would you consider supporting this vision by rolling off the board for this next term? In doing so, you will be creating space for new voices and leadership, both of which are critical to the long-term sustainability of our work.

This would need to be customized and the conversation may require multiple exchanges. No longer serving on the board doesn't mean that person can no longer support the organization's work. There are ongoing ways to serve as donors, volunteers, advisors, and more.

Educate and train your current board of directors.

Before a board can lead the organization in a more liberated direction, education and training are required. Educating your board in the work of diversity and liberation will give you a shared foundation on which to build. One way to do this is to attend a training together and/or hire a racial justice educator to facilitate a learning experience for your team.

Expand your network to find new people.

Research ten or twenty organizations, businesses, or communities with which you can begin building relationships. Look for organizations who serve communities unlike your own and yet have a degree of missional or industry alignment with you.

For example, if you lead a nonprofit serving people experiencing homelessness and you want to diversify your board, build relationships with local shelters, food pantries, churches, foundations, and other service providers. By building relationships with the executive directors and communities supporting these other organizations, you're expanding your network. When the time comes for you to recruit new board members, you will have a broader network of relationships to pull from.

Track these potential partners in a spreadsheet. Find them online, determine the best person to connect with, dig for their email address, and reach out to begin building a relationship. Relationships take time, but they are among the most valuable investments we can make.

ADVOCACY AND JUSTICE

Set aside specific donations for reparations, part one.

In an interview with Tom Lin,[1] president and CEO of a national faith-based organization, he shared about how his team was working to take reparations seriously.

The staff members who work for this organization across the United States fundraise for their salaries. Due to systemic factors, the staff of color (i.e., the Black, Indigenous, and people of color who work for this organization) often struggle to raise enough money to cover their salaries. This has been a long-term challenge for the staff of color and the organization as a whole.

In an effort to remedy this, Tom and his team are exploring what it looks like to earmark large donations specifically to help close this fundraising gap for the staff who face systemic barriers to fundraising. This is an act of repair—utilizing funds generated in part by access and privilege and redirecting those funds to the people who need it most.

Set aside specific donations for reparations, part two.

If your organization doesn't raise money but, rather, makes money by selling services, building a reparations fund is still an option for you. If you are person of privilege, especially racial or gender privilege, then some aspect of your ability to make money is tied to the ways systems create an advantage for you while creating barriers for others. One way to demonstrate your understanding of this, and your desire to make it right, is to earmark a portion of the money you bring in and redistribute it to external communities that have not had access to the same advantages as you. The best way to facilitate this is through partnerships with organizations that serve historically marginalized communities.

I learned this from author and racial justice thought leader Jenny B. Potter. She says, "Do not list it as *donations* but *reparations* but with the honest acknowledgment that what you have monetarily has been built over time in a way that BIPOC (Black, Indigenous, people of color) have been excluded from."[2]

Learn the history of your industry.

Interrogate the history and origin stories of your industry. Has your industry routinely advantaged some while creating barriers for others? Was your industry once closed off to women and people of color? Is your industry currently closed off to women and people of color? This research will give your diversity and liberation more context. This might also be a point of interest to members of your team.

Give paid time off for civic duties, like voting or protesting.

Practicing liberation often includes civic engagements, such as protesting or voting. These are basic rights afforded to those of us who live in the United States of America. One of the best ways you can encourage your team members to be civically engaged, if they so choose, is by making these opportunities accessible in the form of paid leave.

NOTES

Chapter One

1. Sandra Maria Van Opstal, "The Diversity Gap—A New Kind of Leader" [Video], April 20, 2020, https://www.youtube.com /watch?v=WDWndT2MQRw\.

2. Resmaa Menakem, *My Grandmother's Hands: Racialized Trauma and the Pathway to Mending Our Hearts and Bodies* (Las Vegas: Central Recovery Press, 2017).

3. The name has been changed.

4. Seegers, L., Ramarajan, L. (2019). Blacks leading whites. In L. Morgan Roberts, A. Mayo, & D. A. Thomas (Eds.), *Race Work and Leadership: New Perspectives on the Black Experience* (pp. 359-372). Boston, MA: Harvard Business Review Press.

5. McCluney, C.L., Rabelo V.C., (2019). Managing diversity, managing blackness. In L. Morgan Roberts, A. Mayo, & D. A. Thomas (Eds.), *Race Work and Leadership: New Perspectives on the Black Experience* (pp. 373-387). Boston, MA: Harvard Business Review Press.

6. Frances Lee Ansley, "White Supremacy (And What We Should Do About It)," in Richard Delgado and Jean Stefancic, eds., *Critical White Studies: Looking Behind the Mirror* (Philadelphia: Temple University Press, 1997), p. 592.

7. Tema Okun and Kenneth Jones, *Dismantling Racism: A Workbook for Social Change Groups* (dRworks, 2001), https://www.showingup forracialjustice.org/white-supremacy-culture-characteristics.html.

Chapter Two

1. Kira Page, "The 'Problem' Woman of Colour in Nonprofit Organizations," December 12, 2018, https://coco-net.org /problem-woman-colour-nonprofit-organizations/.

2. Kira Page, "The 'Problem' Woman of Colour in Nonprofit Organizations."

3. Kira Page, "The 'Problem' Woman of Colour in Nonprofit Organizations."

4. Thomas, K. Robinson, A.J., Provolt, L., Brown, B.L., (2019). When Black leaders leave. In L. Morgan Roberts, A. Mayo, & D. A. Thomas (Eds.), *Race Work and Leadership: New Perspectives on the Black Experience* (pp. 341-357). Boston, MA: Harvard Business Review Press.

5. Healing, P.F., Broomes A. (2019). Authenticity in the workplace. In L. Morgan Roberts, A. Mayo, & D. A. Thomas (Eds.), *Race Work and Leadership: New Perspectives on the Black Experience* (pp. 135-149). Boston, MA: Harvard Business Review Press.

Chapter Three

1. Pamela Newkirk, *Diversity, Inc.: The Failed Promise of a Billion-Dollar Business* (New York: PublicAffairs [division of Hachette Livre], 2019), pp. 177–78.

2. Newkirk, *Diversity, Inc.*

3. Newkirk, *Diversity, Inc.*

4. Vivian Hunt, Lareina Yee, Sara Prince, Sundiatu Dixon-Fyle, *Delivering Through Diversity* (New York: McKinsey & Company, 2018), https://www.mckinsey.com/business-functions /organization/our-insights/delivering-through-diversity#.

5. McCluney, C.L., Rabelo V.C., (2019). Managing diversity, managing blackness. In L. Morgan Roberts, A. Mayo, & D. A. Thomas (Eds.),

Race Work and Leadership: New Perspectives on the Black Experience (pp. 373-387). Boston, MA: Harvard Business Review Press.

6. Bethaney Wilkinson, *The Diversity Gap:* "A New Kind of Leader with Xavier Ramey," April 20, 2020, https://www.youtube.com /watch?v=iM3yGPyygyY.

7. Robin J. Ely and David A. Thomas, "Cultural Diversity at Work: The Effects of Diversity Perspectives on Work Group Processes and Outcomes." *Administrative Science Quarterly* 46, no. 2 (2001): pp. 229–73, doi:10.2307/2667087.

Chapter Four

1. See the Creative Reaction Lab website, https://www.creative reactionlab.com.

Chapter Five

1. Transforming Culture and Naming Racism in Organizations, facilitated by Jen Willsea and Mattice Haynes, Atlanta, Georgia, April 28, 2020.

2. Patrick Lencioni, *The Advantage: Why Organizational Health Trumps Everything Else in Business* (San Francisco: Jossey-Bass, 2012).

3. Purdie-Greenaway, V., Davidson M.N., (2019). Is D&I about us?. In L. Morgan Roberts, A. Mayo, & D. A. Thomas (Eds.), *Race Work and Leadership: New Perspectives on the Black Experience* (pp. 311-322). Boston, MA: Harvard Business Review Press.

4. https://cdn.theatlantic.com/thumbor/t4pvjoz7Wf91fkWzHoxyxh BDfkM=/media/img/2015/08/26/reparations_2/original.jpg; https://www.nytimes.com/interactive/2020/06/24/magazine /reparations-slavery.html.

5. Washington, E. F., Maese, E., McFeely, S. (2019). Workplace engagement and the glass ceiling. In L. Morgan Roberts, A. Mayo, & D. A. Thomas (Eds.), *Race Work and Leadership: New Perspectives on the Black Experience* (pp. 115-134). Boston, MA: Harvard Business Review Press.

Chapter Six

1. Bethaney Wilkinson, *The Diversity Gap*: "Breaking Up with Racial Isolation with Dr. Michael Emerson," October 4, 2019, https://www.thediversitygap.com/podcast-1/breaking-up-with-racial-isolation.

Chapter Seven

1. M. Scott Peck, *The Road Less Traveled: A New Psychology of Love, Traditional Values and Spiritual Growth* (New York: Simon & Schuster, 2003).
2. Vivian Hunt, Lareina Yee, Sara Prince, Sundiatu Dixon-Fyle, *Delivering Through Diversity* (New York: McKinsey & Company, 2018), https://www.mckinsey.com/business-functions /organization/our-insights/delivering-through-diversity#.
3. Parker J. Palmer, *A Hidden Wholeness: The Journey Toward an Undivided Life: Welcoming the Soul and Weaving Community in a Wounded World* (San Francisco: Jossey-Bass, 2008).
4. Washington, E. F., Maese, E., McFeely, S. (2019). Workplace engagement and the glass ceiling. In L. Morgan Roberts, A. Mayo, & D. A. Thomas (Eds.), *Race Work and Leadership: New Perspectives on the Black Experience* (pp. 115-134). Boston, MA: Harvard Business Review Press.
5. Bethaney Wilkinson, *The Diversity Gap:* "Becoming a Diverse Leader with Sam Collier," September 6, 2019, https://podcasts .apple.com/us/podcast/becoming-a-diverse-leader-w-sam-collier /id1474097384?i=1000448775994.
6. J. Stovall, "How to Get Serious About Diversity and Inclusion in the Workplace" [Video], September 2018, TED Conferences, https://www.youtube.com/watch?v=kvdHqS3ryw0&t=340s.

Chapter Eight

1. *Narrative of Sojourner Truth; a bondswoman of olden time, emancipated by the New York Legislature in the early part of the present century; with a history of her labors and correspondence drawn from her "Book of life."* (Battle Creek, MI, Published for the Author, 1878.)

Appendix C

1. Bethaney Wilkinson, *The Diversity Gap*: "Scaling Diversity Across a National Organization with Tom Lin," May 18, 2020, https://podcasts.apple.com/us/podcast/scaling-diversity-across-national-organization-tom/id1474097384?i=1000474945723.

2. Jenny B. Potter, "Some Next Right Anti-Racist Things," 2020, https://www.instagram.com/p/CCdl_msJf75/.

INDEX

ABOUT THE AUTHOR

Bethaney Wilkinson is a writer, leader, and social entrepreneur who has dedicated more than a decade to exploring the intersections of community, racial justice, and social change.

Bethaney began her career as cofounder of Atlanta Harvest, a high-production development farm on a mission to create jobs and strengthen economies in disadvantaged communities. She then founded G.Race Dialogues, a faith and community-based initiative designed to support individuals and organizations pursuing racial reconciliation. Bethaney expanded her research and broadened her reach after joining the team at Plywood People, a nonprofit in Atlanta leading a community of startups doing good.

As part of her work in diversity and cultural change, Bethaney is an invited speaker at major conferences and top global companies. She is the host of the popular podcast *The Diversity Gap* and is the founder of The Diversity Gap Academy, an online learning platform for leaders seeking to pair their good intentions for diversity with true cultural change.